REPRESENTING AFRICA
IN CHILDREN'S
LITERATURE

How Picturebooks Work
by Maria Nikolajeva and Carole Scott

Brown Gold
Milestones of African American Children's Picture Books, 1845–2002
by Michelle H. Martin

Russell Hoban/Forty Years
Essays on His Writing for Children
by Alida Allison

Apartheid and Racism in South African Children's Literature
by Donnarae MacCann and Amadu Maddy

Empire's Children
Empire and Imperialism in Classic British Children's Books
by M. Daphne Kutzer

Constructing the Canon of Children's Literature
Beyond Library Walls and Ivory Towers
by Anne Lundin

Youth of Darkest England
Working Class Children at the Heart of Victorian Empire
by Troy Boone

Ursula K. Leguin Beyond Genre
Literature for Children and Adults
by Mike Cadden

Twice-Told Children's Tales
edited by Betty Greenway

Diana Wynne Jones
The Fantastic Tradition and Children's Literature
by Farah Mendlesohn

Childhood and Children's Books in Early Modern Europe, 1550–1800
edited by Andrea Immel and Michael Witmore

Voracious Children
Who Eats Whom in Children's Literature
by Carolyn Daniel

National Character in South African Children's Literature
by Elwyn Jenkins

Myth, Symbol, and Meaning in *Mary Poppins*
The Governess as Provocateur
by Georgia Grilli

A Critical History of French Children's Literature
by Penny Brown

The Gothic in Children's Literature
Haunting the Borders
Edited by Anna Jackson, Karen Coats, and Roderick McGillis

Reading Victorian Schoolrooms
Childhood and Education in Nineteenth-Century Fiction
by Elizabeth Gargano

Soon Come Home to This Island
West Indians in British Children's Literature
by Karen Sands-O'Connor

Boys in Children's Literature and Popular Culture
Masculinity, Abjection, and the Fictional Child
by Annette Wannamaker

Into the Closet
Cross-dressing and the Gendered Body in Children's Literature
by Victoria Flanagan

Russian Children's Literature and Culture
edited by Marina Balina and Larissa Rudova

The Outside Child In and Out of the Book
by Christine Wilkie-Stibbs

Representing Africa in Children's Literature
Old and New Ways of Seeing
by Vivian Yenika-Agbaw

REPRESENTING AFRICA IN CHILDREN'S LITERATURE

Old and New Ways of Seeing

VIVIAN YENIKA-AGBAW

Routledge
Taylor & Francis Group

NEW YORK AND LONDON

First published 2008
by Routledge
270 Madison Ave, New York, NY 10016

Simultaneously published in the UK
by Routledge
2 Park Square, Milton Park, Abingdon, Oxon OX14 4RN

Routledge is an imprint of the Taylor & Francis Group, an informa business

© 2008 Taylor & Francis

Typeset in Minion by Kestroke, 28 High Street, Tettenhall, Wolverhampton
Printed and bound in the United States of America on acid-free paper by
Sheridan Books, Inc.

All rights reserved. No part of this book may be reprinted or reproduced or utilized in
any form or by any electronic, mechanical, or other means, now known or hereafter
invented, including photocopying and recording, or in any information storage or
retrieval system, without permission in writing from the publishers.

Trademark Notice: Product or corporate names may be trademarks or registered
trademarks, and are used only for identification and explanation without intent to
infringe.

Library of Congress Cataloging in Publication Data
Yenika-Agbaw, Vivian S.
Representing Africa in children's literature : old and new ways of seeing / Vivian
Yenika-Agbaw.
p. cm. — (Children's literature and culture ; 50)
Includes bibliographical references and index.
1. Children's literature—History and criticism. 2. Africans in literature.
3. Africa—In literature. I. Title.
PN1009.5.A47Y46 2008
809′.93326—dc22
2007017603

ISBN 10: 0–415–97468–2 (hbk)
ISBN 10: 0–203–93516–0 (ebk)

ISBN 13: 978–0–415–97468–4 (hbk)
ISBN 13: 978–0–203–93516–3 (ebk)

AUGUSTANA LIBRARY
UNIVERSITY OF ALBERTA

To my children

Contents

Series Editor's Foreword

Dedicated to furthering original research in children's literature and culture, the Children's Literature and Culture series includes monographs on individual authors and illustrators, historical examinations of different periods, literary analyses of genres, and comparative studies on literature and the mass media. The series is international in scope and is intended to encourage innovative research in children's literature with a focus on interdisciplinary methodology.

Children's literature and culture are understood in the broadest sense of the term *children* to encompass the period of childhood up through adolescence. Owing to the fact that the notion of childhood has changed so much since the origination of children's literature, this Routledge series is particularly concerned with transformations in children's culture and how they have affected the representation and socialization of children. While the emphasis of the series is on children's literature, all types of studies that deal with children's radio, film, television, and art are included in an endeavor to grasp the aesthetics and values of children's culture. Not only have there been momentous changes in children's culture in the last fifty years, but there have been radical shifts in the scholarship that deals with these changes. In this regard, the goal of the Children's Literature and Culture series is to enhance research in this field and, at the same time, point to new directions that bring together the best scholarly work throughout the world.

Jack Zipes

Acknowledgments

I wish to thank Dan Hade for exposing me to the scholarship of Children's Literature, and Patrick Shannon for instilling in me a passion for social justice and an interest in postcolonial studies. I would also like to thank Jane and Rufus Blanshard for their non-stop support—moral and otherwise—of my academic/ professional career in the United States since 1984. My husband, Steven Ekema Agbaw, and children, Yenik, Luma and Joy also deserve a special thanks for their patience, and constant support.

In addition, I am grateful for permission to reprint four essays originally published in national journals, and an extract:

"Images of West Africa in Children's Books: Replacing Old Stereotypes with New Ones?" *The New Advocate* 11.3 (1998): 203–218.

"Illustrations and the Messages They Convey: African Culture in Picture Books," *Sankofa: Journal of African Children's and Young Adult Literature* 4 (2005): 35–46.

"Revising Traditional Cultural Practices in Two Picture Book Versions of African Folktales," *Bookbird* 3 (2005): 18–24.

"Individual Healing vs. Communal Healing: Three African Girls' Attempt at Constructing Unique Identities," *Children's Literature Association Quarterly* 27.3 (2002): 121–128 [reprinted by permission of the Children's Literature Association].

"The Village in the Modern World: Children's Literature About West Africa," *Teaching and Learning Literature* 5.4 (1996): 2–7.

Introduction

RECORDS

Once a black child has an arrest
RECORD
or
a
RECORD of low grades in school
or
a RECORD as a troublemaker
or
a RECORD as a mentally disturbed child—

The RECORD haunts our children the rest of their lives, keeping them
from getting ahead, shattering their aspirations and dreams forever.

(The Great Blacks in Wax Museum)

Culture is the practice and beliefs of a particular group of people, which distinguish them from all other groups through material and symbolic forms. As Hunt (1993) explains, "the cultural transmission of symbolic forms" enables groups to represent themselves to their group members and the outside world (p. 13). Once made public, these symbols become the sole means through which most of the world comes to know any particular culture. In this way, the power to control the symbolic representations has dramatic repercussions for the relative status of one's culture vis-à-vis other cultures in the world, Africa included.

African cultural symbols have greatly influenced the artistic forms of most cultures in the world; cultural artifacts from different parts of Africa also continue to fill Western museums. And several scholars have established connections among music and dance steps in the West with their African origin. For example, Thompson (1990) traces the popular African American jazz, the Brazilian music, samba, and the Cuban dance, rumba to Central Africa. Philips (1990) has made a connection between the banjo music and its West African origin. Despite this diversity, popular media in the West often represent Africa as a homogenous enigma, which defies modernization, even civilization. These representations do little to enhance understanding of African cultures, and less to increase the worldly status of members of these groups.

Consequently, Africans are perceived by the outside world as children who need to be constantly told what to do, and how to do it; they continue to live under perpetual threat and patronage from their Western benefactors. Understandably, Africans then cannot necessarily remain on the sideline and watch the rest of the world make decisions about their fate without feeling upset, or outright angry. This may be because there was a time in their historical past when they participated actively in defining who they were, and in shaping their own destiny. However, this was during pre-colonial times—long before they encountered the Europeans.

Pre-colonial Africa then according to Du Bois (1992), although not perfect, was a time when Africans had dignity and commanded respect from outsiders. This respect for Africans and their culture became nonexistent soon after the Europeans arrived in the continent. Thus:

> There came to Africa an end of industry especially guided by taste and art. Cheap European goods pushed in and threw the native products out of competition [...] Methods of work were lost and forgotten [...] The old religion was held up to ridicule, the old culture and ethical standards degraded or disappeared and gradually all over Africa spread the inferiority complex, the fear of color, the worship of white skin, the imitation of white ways of doing and thinking whether good, bad or indifferent. By the end of the nineteenth century the degradation of Africa was as complete as organized human means could make it. (Du Bois, 1992, p. 78)

This state of affairs continues right into the twenty-first century in different ways. *Our* political survival depends on the whims of the West; *our* educational systems are tailored after the Europeans'. Even our art form has evolved to the point where it is hard to tell what is authentic (African) anymore.

This would not have mattered much if African children were spared this cultural confusion. However, it is not so. They are not only part of different African communities, but they are now members of a global culture susceptible to cultural images from media and other sources, including literature that undermines their heritage in blatant or subtle ways. As concerned individuals try to rectify the situation by filling in gaps with stories of African childhood, they produce books whose cultural content may be questionable. However, because the majority of African children may not have access to these books, they are denied the opportunity to examine these cultural experiences and either agree with the depiction of their culture, or question/challenge inappropriate images of themselves that they may find. They therefore remain doubly marginalized.

Do existing books about African children and youth capture the complexity of their experiences as Africans, children, and human beings? This is what I attempt to answer in the eleven chapters included in this collection.

I have included three chapters that examine the images of Africa prevalent in books, four chapters that address gender issues, and four chapters that deal with literacy and cultural survival. The majority of the chapters are about West African cultures, partly because my primary area of research interest is post-independence West African literature for children and young adults. However, more than ten distinct African countries are represented here; two stories are set in generic African countries, two in several African countries, and eleven, which are set in the diaspora, do make reference to either generic Africa or to a particular African culture. I examined this set of books because of the African-American connection with Africa. It seems fitting to do so because throughout the history of human civilization the notion of blackness, which implies race, has consistently been linked to power. "Race," as Goldberg (1993) notes,

> has been a constitutive feature of modernity, ordering conceptions of self and other, of sociopolitical membership and exclusions. It has identified exploitable individuals and populations for subjection and it has been used to rationalize and legitimate domination, subjugation, even extermination. (p. 148)

Blackness as the racial identity of a group of people has played a crucial role in shaping global historical events. Rejecting their position as a racial Other to White supremacist subjects, for some, blackness then becomes a cultural identity that provides the platform from which they can fight domination (Marable, 1992). In the course of creating this new identity that would deconstruct the way Blacks have been and are still perceived by the dominant Other, a link is forged with Africa whereby Africanism begins to inform the whole notion of blackness and vice versa (Diawara, 1992).

More than 125 books, representing six genres, are either discussed extensively or made reference to in this collection. These genres include concept books, folktales, poetry, biography, short stories, and novels.

Despite the controversy over the use of the English language in works considered to be African literature, all the chapters here are limited to books written in this language. As Irele (1995) observes, "[o]ur expression in the European languages has not only functioned as a mode of contestation of the colonial ideology but also served an emancipatory project" (p. 18). When considered in this light European languages cease to be oppressive, but become a tool of subversion used for liberating purposes.

The books discussed here are written by Africans, African-Americans, and Whites. This collection will add to the dialogue on the state of African children's literature in our global community and in the academia, which Nancy J. Schmidt

(1975, 1989), Meena Khorana (1994, 1998), Osayimwense Osa (1995), Raoul Granqvist and Jurgen Martini (1997), and Donnarae MacCann and Yulisa Amadu Maddy (MacCann & Maddy, 1996; McCann, 2001) have been engaged in for almost three decades. As Khorana explained to me at a children's literature conference at Calgary, Canada in 1999, we, children's literature scholars, have to give African children's literature the scholarly attention it deserves, instead of only providing information about books that exist or not, and pointing out problems about publishing in Africa and for Africans. Osa (1998) echoes this sentiment somewhat in his review of Granqvist and Martini's *Preserving the Landscape of the Imagination: Children's Literature in Africa* (1997), when he remarks that "the reader seeking an in-depth reading, understanding or illumination of a specific or particular genre of African children's literature in this book will be disappointed" (p. 170). He also notes that

> while it is worthwhile to have a book of comprehensive information about children's literature in Africa, without caution, it risks becoming a patchwork that attempts all inclusiveness of breadth and scope in English, in French, or in African languages of all the literary forms—major and minor—in African children's literature. (p. 170)

I share this view in a sense because I strongly believe it is almost impossible to accomplish this feat with Africa being as large a continent as it is, with multiple realities/cultures even within particular regions in different nations.

Thus although the chapters in this book explore literature from and about several African countries and include literature from six genres or subgenres, the scope is still limited. For example, I did not include any sections on children's drama. To understand the amount of work that lies ahead of us regarding African children's literature, all one needs to do is go over the three annotated bibliographies by Schmidt (1975, 1989), and Khorana (1994); and of course, as Osayimwense postulates, "[t]here's no bibliography that thoroughly covers children's literature about Africa in one European or African language" (p. 170).

This notwithstanding, it is our collective responsibility as Africanist scholars to examine those we have access to critically. In a way Achebe (1995) insists on this when he remarks that

> it is because our own critics have been somewhat hesitant in taking control of our literary criticism [. . .] that the task has fallen to others, some of whom [. . .] have been excellent and sensitive. And yet most of what remains to be done can best be tackled by ourselves. If we fall back, can we complain that others are rushing forward? (p. 61)

Encouraged by these words of wisdom, I take the plunge, knowing full well that the road to criticism can be bumpy. I welcome dialogue, for I know that my essays, which vary in length and focus, may not have definitive answers to some of the issues raised in the books about African children and adolescents. If they draw attention to these issues, I believe I would have accomplished a significant part of my goal.

The main limitation of the collection is that the books discussed are available primarily in the West. I do not claim that African children have access to these books; neither do I conclude that the books can be found in all Western classrooms. I can only stipulate that because they exist, chances are some children have either read them, or will eventually do so; and some teachers may be using them already, or eventually.

The frameworks I use to discuss issues are also subjective. The primary analytical framework, however, is cultural studies (postcolonial and womanist/feminist). This means that there are other aspects of the books that I might not have focused on thoroughly, or that I might have privileged theory and ideology more to shape my interpretations of the different texts.

The book is divided into three sections and an afterword: Part 1 focuses on images; Part 2 re-examines tradition and gender issues; Part 3 raises the question of literacy and African cultural survival, and the afterword focuses on publishing challenges and the apparent or possible hybrid nature of literature about African children and young adults. Each chapter has been presented in some version, at one point in time as papers at international, national, regional, or local conferences. Five have already appeared in reputable journals.

In Chapter 1, I discuss four distinct images prevalent in selected books (fiction) published after 1960 by African and Western authors. This essay has been reprinted three times. In this chapter I discuss the challenges Africans and Blacks face when writing about African children, for there seems to be a popular belief that "all" insiders can tell authentic stories. In Chapter 2, I focus exclusively on the messages of Africa conveyed through illustrations by four renowned Western illustrators, three of whom are identified as being among the most popular picture book authors/illustrators in the United States (McElmeel, 2000). Because a picture book is defined primarily by format, the genres examined here range from alphabet books to historical realism.

In Chapter 3 I dwell on the images of Africa prevalent in books (genres that did not feature in my discussion in Chapter 1) that target young children in grades K–3. I conclude this chapter by discussing the subtle messages communicated about Africa and Africans through folktales.

Chapters 4 through 7 deal more with tradition and gender issues. I open this section by comparing two girls' childhood experiences in two distinct African communities as I argue that religion plays a great role in the way parents, especially fathers, raise their children. Because of the bulk of African children's folktales that exist in print, in Chapter 5, I look at different ways two authors have revised traditional practices and gender roles in African village communities. I argue here that it is a good start since it shows that our culture is not necessarily static, as many may be tempted to believe. In Chapters 6 and 7, I examine the different ways young females struggle to adapt in modern and traditional African communities as they deal with their sexuality vis-à-vis colonialism and patriarchy.

The last set of chapters explores issues of literacy and cultural empowerment. In Chapter 8, I discuss resistant images in a controversial picture book as I establish the connections between Blacks in Africa and Blacks in the diaspora. Chapter 9 explores African sites of cultural memory prevalent in African-American literature. Identifying literary works by African-Americans that use the African continent as a site of memory enables me to show how Blacks in the West fall back on their cultural heritage for strength to deal with the constant struggle against social injustice encountered in a white, racist, and capitalist society. Chapter 10 addresses the need for more quality picture books to be written and published by Africans. For this may eventually prevent us from being "culturally dependent" on industrialized Western nations as Altbach (1995) has observed. I conclude with a chapter on the hybrid nature of what many may consider as "African children's literature."

It is my hope that these essays will provoke thought, and generate dialogue among scholars of African literature, children's and young adult literature, publishers of children's books, teachers, and government officials as we all seek ways to guide our children to make better decisions about their lives and future. African children are worthy of our attention, time, and money. We should not betray their trust!

Part I
Image Making and Children's Books

For people who have been nearly invisible or made the object of ridicule, the image-maker has the vast potential for changing their world by changing both the way they see themselves and the way they are seen by others.

(Rudine Sims, *Shadow and Substance*, 1982)

Chapter One
Images of West Africa in Children's Books: Replacing Old Stereotypes with New Ones?

> Indeed, Africa for some Americans, is one vast exotic place, perhaps
> a single gigantic country where wild animals roam and where people
> cannot resist killing and perhaps eating each other.
>
> (Ungar, *Africa: The People and Politics of an*
> *Emerging Continent*, 1986)

Western interest in non-Western cultures increased as European colonialism declined in Africa and other parts of the world. For many Westerners, movies, television, and stories are the most popular means of obtaining information about these cultures. These different art forms, particularly stories written for children and young adults, enable Western readers to develop certain visions of life in other parts of the world.

Film as a popular medium transmits cultural images that shape viewers' perceptions of a group of people. These images, whether good or bad, come to define a cultural group and become stereotypes through which outsiders recognize and talk about people from that particular culture. While movies such as *King Solomon's Mines* (1937), *Congo* (1995), and *I Dreamed of Africa* (2000) represent a stereotypical image of Africa as violent and primitive, *Out of Africa* (1986) celebrates Africa as a natural and romantic place, thus perpetuating another stereotype. Television news reports often depict Africa as a continent ridden with killer diseases that might someday wipe out every human soul on this earth or as a continent plagued by famine. These art forms invent realities for how Africans are defined in our global community. In this chapter, I discuss the cultural authenticity of the portrayal of West Africa in fiction for children and young adults. Because there is little research on African representation in children's literature, the precise images that dominate this genre are not known despite the popular belief that these images are largely negative (Khorana, 1994). I decided to focus on images because people tend to believe the images of themselves and others as portrayed in print and mass media (hooks, 1995, 1994). Children can be manipulated by these images to accept their positions in society as communicated by symbolic forms.

My discussion of images and cultural authenticity is framed within a postcolonial theoretical perspective. Postcolonial theory deconstructs colonial ideologies of power that privilege Western cultural practices (Giroux, 1992), challenges the historical representations of colonized groups (Adam & Tiffin, 1990), and gives voice to those at that margin (Spivak, 1990). Postcolonial theory thus provides a framework through which scholars can identify and resist subtle and blatant social injustices. By examining the cultural authenticity of children's books written by Western and indigenous authors, it becomes easier to uncover signs of domination that perpetuate unequal power distribution among nations (Ashcroft, Griffiths, & Tiffin, 1995a).

I have limited myself to West African experiences in this chapter because Africa is a vast continent with varied cultural practices. Also, I am more familiar with some of the cultural practices that exist in that part of the continent because I was born and raised in Cameroon, a country in West Africa. Cameroon, like most West African countries, has villages, towns, and cities, as well as a variety of socio-ethnic cultural practices.

Identifying Children's Books

Fifty children's books set in West Africa were identified using Khorana's (1994) *Africa in Literature for Children and Young Adults.* I examined books written after 1960 because this is the era when most African nations won their independence and presumably left colonialism. Also, this era is when "the history of literature written and published specifically for African children began" (Khorana, 1994, p. xxix).

I focused on K–12 fiction set in West Africa because fiction captures an author's version of what really is, what used to be, and what ought to be. I included fiction by African, African-American, and White authors in order to understand what these authors believe are the significant and authentic African cultural experiences worth sharing with their audiences.

When looking at each book, I first examined the settings and the characters. Since West Africa is composed of several countries and ethnic groups whose colonial histories overlap or differ at times, I paid attention to the socioeconomic practices of the characters. For example, I read to find out if the setting was rural, urban, or semi-urban/rural. Such elements as the kinds of houses/huts that dominate the setting, the economic and cultural activities in the community, and the surrounding environment were crucial in my interpretation of setting. I also read texts and pictures to determine the main characters. If the main characters were human beings, I looked at age and gender to understand what or whose experience was important to the different authors. I considered the different themes in a storyline and examined any dialogue between characters. Knowing that the dialogue generally could not be authentic since most of it was rendered in English, a foreign language, I searched for the meaning behind the ideas and messages these characters communicated to each other. In this chapter, I limit my discussion to fifteen books randomly selected from the different analytical categories that emerged out of the data on the fifty books.

I found that children's books published after 1960 continue to represent West Africa as either primitive/barbaric or natural/romantic. These images have also been used to define other cultures that underwent the colonial experience. Tugend (1997) observed that Africans, Indians, and Chinese are portrayed as "savages" in British children's literature (p. Al2). Even in the United States, Native Americans are constantly defined through this colonial lens (Slapin & Seale, 1992). With this trend in children's books, it is necessary to raise issues of cultural authenticity and to identify the colonial markers that negate non-Western cultures.

WEST AFRICA AS PRIMITIVE/BARBARIC

As in popular media, one recurrent image in these books is that of Africa as a primitive/barbaric place, an image that is neocolonial. The stories are set in either the jungle or a village and depict West Africa as barbaric with people whose survival methods seem ridiculous and primitive. The "natives" fight with animals in a capricious jungle for their basic needs, and the "nonnatives" live in constant fear of being attacked by animals and barbaric natives.

Barbaric Images

In Ekwensi's *Juju Rock* (1966), fifteen-year-old Rikku goes with European gold seekers in an attempt to win a scholarship to a British university. As they approach their destination, a remote village, he must risk his life for them and so shaves his head to look like a "primitive" villager. Rikku manifests a neocolonial attitude when he describes West Africans as having unusual hairstyles and tribal marks that make them look and act in frightening ways. Rikku remarks, "We were regarded as spies, intruders to be sacrificed" (p. 68). Like a typical loyal servant, he plans to save his White masters from West African savages, even though he is aware that these White men have plans to dispose of him after the gold mine expedition.

Ekwensi, a Nigerian, depicts West Africans as barbaric and dangerous. According to Osa (1995), Ekwensi later revised *Juju Rock* because of its overt similarity to adventure stories written by European colonialists. Osa (1995) also comments that *Juju Rock* was "primarily a book of entertainment rather than moral value" (p. 20). To me, the novel oppresses as it entertains.

Pete Watson's *The Heart of the Lion* (2005) also depicts West Africa as primitive. This picture book chronicles all that the white narrator may perceive as "weird" about West Africa. After reading the first vignette the reader may be tempted to pass the story off as a romantic image of Africa; however, on further reading one notices that Watson's view even of one village is extremely limited. This is because in a book that seems more like an album of strange happenings in an African village where the White male narrator lives with his parents, daily occurrences are either exotic or frightening. The only functional African he integrates in the story is Yampabou and we meet him only after the narrator has introduced us to three elephants that "connect in a parade" (unpaged). It is this "local" boy who takes the young White boy along, showing him "a world of mysteries and magic" (unpaged). This West African world includes eccentric people who play with scorpions, make poison, eat strange meats, torture animals and insects, and believe in magic. It also includes characters like Yampabou, whose "filed" pointed teeth make him look like a "jack-o-lantern," and other characters who suffer from various infirmities (unpaged). Like Watson's *The Market Lady and the Mango Tree* (1994) that depicts ridiculous images of West Africa (Benin), the idea for the story stems out of his experience as a Peace Corps Volunteer.

Ekwensi's and Watson's books without doubt reinforce the image of Africa as barbaric or primitive. Ironically, both have White characters who are being escorted around by an African guide, and it is these guides who somehow lend credibility to the primitive images.

Ridiculous Survival Methods

Gray's *A Country Far Away* (1989) and Olaleye's *Bitter Bananas* (1994) explore the hardship of life in West Africa. Gray compares the life of an African boy living in a village to that of a White boy growing up in a town. Although the text explores the universals of working, eating, and playing, it is evident that the White world is much better. Gray constantly compares the hardship of the African boy's life in a remote village to the comfort of the White boy's modern urban world. The author's depiction of the hard life in West Africa makes it an unpleasant alternative to life in the West.

The story opens: "Today was an ordinary day. I stayed at home" (unpaged). This text is flanked by two illustrations—one of a West African village and one of a Western suburban town. The great disparity in the two boys' lifestyles is immediately evident and continues throughout the book. The West African boy works hard in the fields as a goat herder, whereas the White boy washes a car in their driveway. Washing a car is work, no doubt, but it is trivial compared to herding goats in the wilderness. The West African boy carries items on his shoulders, climbs a coconut tree to tap palm wine, and rides a donkey home from school. The White boy vacuums the carpet, pushes dirt in a wheelbarrow, and rides a bus home from school.

Gray highlights these differences through illustrations that communicate the material deprivation prevalent in the West African boy's lifestyle (Khorana, 1994). Afolayan, Kuntz, and Naze (1992) support this critique but suggest that "this book means well" (p. 421). Though it may mean well, the author inadvertently equates materialism with superiority. From a postcolonial perspective Gray flaunts the superior ways of Western civilization over African "primitive" ways of survival. A fair comparison would have been to compare urban life and children from similar socioeconomic backgrounds in both regions. Instead, the story perpetuates colonization by depicting Africa as a primitive place.

Olaleye's picture book *Bitter Bananas* (1994) goes one step further by perpetuating the stereotype of Africans fighting for space and food with animals. The author, although writing from an insider's perspective as a Nigerian, depicts a hero who spends too much physical and mental energy chasing baboons off his "palm sap." Through hard work and ingenuity, Yusuf finally figures out a way to outsmart the baboons. This picture book reminds me of movies like *The Gods Must be Crazy* (1986) and *Congo* (1995). Africans are reduced to objects of entertainment—primitive people who must struggle to live and whose survival methods look ridiculous. According to these texts, to labor in West Africa is to work for little material reward.

Africa as a Capricious Jungle

Zimelman's *Treed by a Pride of Irate Lions* (1990) captures the image of Africa as a capricious jungle. The father, a White man, goes to Africa to see if wild animals will appreciate him, because he believes that domestic animals are "too refined for a man like me" (unpaged). He is rejected violently by the wild animals in West Africa. Father needs to control something and sees his opportunity in West Africa, a body of land that has a history of colonial domination. Throughout his stay in West Africa, he does not interact with any human being. Africa is stereotyped as a jungle populated by wild animals, a place of violence and danger.

This image is also echoed in Steig's *Doctor De Soto Goes to Africa* (1992). Doctor De Soto, a dentist, accepts an invitation to help an elephant with a tooth problem in Africa. In West Africa, a baboon that "emigrated" from India and that resents the elephant for calling him a "moron" kidnaps Doctor De Soto. This is an interesting twist that reflects a colonial lens. Although the main character survives this experience, he returns home with an image of Africa as a dangerous place. "Doctor De Soto lay on his back, saying his wife's name over and over and wishing he'd never seen Africa, never even heard of it" (unpaged).

These two books communicate the image of Africa as being dangerous to foreigners. To render professional services to West Africa is to put one's life in jeopardy.

Insider Stereotypes of West Africa as Barbaric

The books that portray West Africa as barbaric perpetuate West Africa's supposed inferiority related to the West through characters and settings that are primitive, harsh, and dangerous. These books, two of which are written by West Africans, depict West Africa as a place where people fight for space and food with animals as they struggle to survive in a materially deprived environment.

There are explanations as to why insiders, particularly those who have lived through colonial experiences, would inadvertently perpetuate stereotypes of their culture. Zipes (1993) notes that because writers are part of our society, their works are not free from the hegemony that perpetuates dominant ideological practices. Both Ekwensi and Olaleye have other texts that are not neocolonial.

These shifts among West African writers may indicate their internal struggles with the ideologies of empowerment, oppression, and liberation. Postcolonial theory acknowledges this struggle, but emphasizes the need to identify overt and subtle signs of domination that keep an individual from completely liberating himself or herself from the bondage and cycle of oppression. As Fee (1995) notes, "Rewriting the dominant ideology is not easy" (p. 245); however, it is my hope that West African authors will not give up their attempts at depicting our multiple realities.

WEST AFRICA AS ROMANTIC

The other dominant image of Africa, nature and romance, comes through the works of Black (African and American) authors and those of White authors. I have decided to divide this discussion into two sub-categories because this image is interpreted differently in the works of these two groups of writers. The Black authors glorify their *cultural heritage and past traditions*, whereas their White counterparts emphasize the exotic nature of West African cultural practices and the *universal truths* of human experience.

Black Authors' Romantic Images of West Africa

Black authors depict a romantic image through Afrocentric literature that promotes racial solidarity/liberation and cultural pride and treats Africans as subjects. These stories are set in pre-colonial, contemporary, or implied West African villages. Advocates of this view consider the communal life in the village to be superior to the individualistic quest for materialism that is pervasive in towns (Asante, 1985; Chinweizu, Onwuchekwa, & Madubuike, 1983).

The authors depict cultural experiences that affirm Africans as brave warriors who take pride in their ancestral past; as people who were/are actively involved in cultural practices, which was/is more worthy because it emphasizes communal living over individualistic quest for material goods; and as people who should not tolerate any form of injustice within their village community. The plots rotate around West African traditional village cultural practices, and the themes include cultural pride, injustice, and industry

Traditional Village Cultural Practices as the Standard

Mendez's *The Black Snowman* (1989) explores the struggle of being Black and poor in a White plentiful society. Jacob hates being Black and poor. His faith in himself and his people is restored when a Black snowman takes him to an imaginary Ghanaian kingdom to show him what his African ancestors contributed to world civilization. The snowman tells him, "These are strong, brave Africans from whom you descend, Black people who should make you proud of your heritage," and encourages him to "believe in your strength" (unpaged). Although Black children need these words of wisdom, Mendez stereotypes West Africa as a romantic pre-colonial village with thriving kingdoms and brave warriors.

Franklin's *The Old, Old Man and the Very Little Boy* (1992) emphasizes village cultural pride through an intergenerational link between the elderly and the young, who are torn between the old and new ways of doing things. Using an oral storytelling technique with an old man as the storyteller, Franklin describes the accomplishments of great West African warriors of the past. The young boy prepares himself for his future role as a brave warrior through these stories by recognizing the role and cultural practices of the African male within a village setting. The hunting culture is handed down to a new generation of young men who are being prepared for their roles as protectors of the village. Good though this may be, hunting alone can no longer sustain life in contemporary villages, especially with the new awareness of animal preservation.

Communal Life

Easmon's *Bisi and the Golden Disc* (1990) explores marriage within a royal kingdom in a pre-colonial village. Although Bisi is in love with Akin, her father (the king) wants her to marry a magician who will make him more powerful. The village community is involved in the courtship as Bisi's attendants help locate Akin. Easmon emphasizes communal lifestyles in her depiction of the marriage ritual within this village community. Because she is writing from an Afrocentric perspective, she portrays life in a pre-colonial village as being harmonious, with the rich living happily together with the not-so-rich. This peace is briefly disturbed by the use of magic and greed. Nonetheless, things work out well in the end.

Power relations in this community are glossed over quickly. Thus even though Bisi is a princess, her "six attendants were like sisters to her" (unpaged). Bisi, however, does not hesitate to treat them as servants when the need arises. Although pre-colonial communal cultural practices were good, they were not necessarily free from oppression.

Ekeh's *How Tables Came to Umu Madu* (1989) parodies the uncritical attachment of Africans to material things introduced by White folks. The author becomes didactic as he shows how this obsession with material goods destroys an otherwise harmonious community. All is peaceful in the pre-colonial West African village until a White man, No Skin, appears and donates one table to the entire community. Envy and pride enter the village as "those who ate at the table stuck up their noses in the air and looked down on those who ate on the ground" (p. 15). Even when the table is destroyed, individual villagers never return to eating on the ground.

No Skin's introduction of a material culture into the village where communal cultural practices had been going on for decades makes the villagers materialistic and individualistic. "Young men refused to yield to their elders. Young women became very haughty and refused to get married" (p. 55). Ekeh contrasts the harmony that pervaded the pre-colonial village with the turbulence of the colonial and postcolonial era. In doing so, he reduces the cultural experience to the popular stereotype of villagers having no differences of opinion with one another.

From a postcolonial stance, these books communicate that West African Blacks are guaranteed a peaceful existence only if they adhere to the traditional practices of long ago. For spiritual strength to face the challenge of living in an unjust society, the characters in these stories must adopt West African village cultural practices. Unfortunately, present-day problems are not that easy to define.

White Authors' Romantic Images of West Africa

White authors capture the dominant image of nature and romance through literature that I categorize as postcolonial Western literature. This literature continues to colonize by dominating others in a subtle manner as it affirms a particular cultural experience. On the one hand, such literature acknowledges the existence of West African cultural experiences, but it simultaneously maintains a tone of skepticism as to the qualitative value of such cultural experience. It connotes what Sims (1983) describes as the culture being " a half-empty cup" (p. 651), meaning that the culture lacks substance. The setting for this type of literature is predominantly rural or semi-rural.

Universal "Truths"

Appiah's adolescent novel, *The Gift of the Mmoatia* (1972), explores the friendship between two girls—one English and the other Ghanaian. They seem to have many things in common, including a belief in mmoatia or fairies. The characters move back and forth between urban and rural communities in both England and Ghana. When these two girls first meet, what strikes them most is each other's color. Anne Marie sees Abena as "very dark—almost black" with "short curly black hair like a boy's" (p. 7). Abena notices that Anne Marie is "very fair and has blue eyes, and is the same age as me" (p. 11). Both girls come from traditional families with affectionate grandmothers who know about the "little people" who live in the bushes. The story seeks to reassure the children that "it doesn't matter if you are black or white."

Subtle forms of colonial domination manifest themselves in this text. For example, Abena's mmoatia are "little people" who are "dark like me or red coloured" (p. 23). Anne Marie's fairies are simply "little men" with "small wrinkled faces full of smiles" (p. 89). While waiting for her mother to be cured in a hospital in England, and staying with Anne Marie's grandmother, Abena is enthralled by the beauty and abundance of the English garden flowers. Appiah confirms her ignorance and enchantment, stating, "English flowers did not do well in Ghana, and most gardens only had only a few kinds. Others were either burnt up by the hot sun or broken down by the torrential rains" (p. 62). My reading of this is that although Ghana is fine as a country, its harsh climate deters nature's beauty.

Even though Appiah tries to make the friendship equal, it is the Ghanaian family that profits materially and culturally from the relationship. Yes, White people can be friends with Africans, but Black people end up becoming the White man's burden. They can also benefit more from the superior cultural environment that the West provides.

Grifalconi's Osa's *Pride* (1990) explores the universal experience of being proud. Told in the first person, Osa is viewed as stubborn in her belief that her father who had participated in the "big war" will return home. Her stubbornness leads her to become full of "foolish pride" and to lose her friends. All ends well when her grandmother brings her attention to her behavior. Osa's voice throughout the book sounds more like that of a child from the United States than a Cameroonian girl.

Although Grifalconi's illustrations are exquisite, her theme of universal truth results in the book lacking a storyline. It is a story about generic human experiences being passed off as a story about West Africa. Because of its focus on the universal theme of "foolish pride," the story could be set anywhere, and so indigenous West African cultural practices are overlooked. From a postcolonial stance, I believe that it renders West African culture invisible and so maintains Grifalconi's superiority as a Western writer over the subject she chooses to write about.

Cowen-Fletcher's *It Takes a Village* (1994), a beautiful picture book that tells the story of a market woman who entrusts her young son to the care of her slightly older daughter, Yemi, for one day also echoes a romantic image of West Africa. Africa, to the author, is a place where children can wander off on their own without a care. Although the story is charming and the illustrations are exquisite, as Cowen-Fletcher shows how a community can come together to look after a child, she inadvertently also communicates that West African parents can be irresponsible. Looking at this picture book closely, the first thing that strikes me is the absence of parent figures on the jacket cover. Throughout the book there's no place where she mentions the children's father. Neither does he feature in any of the illustrations. Africa is then a big playground where parents do not really matter.

Ashcroft, Griffiths, and Tiffin (1995b) argue that universalism and the notion of a unitary and homogenous human nature serve to marginalize and exclude. When authors capture the universal experience of humankind in children's literature, they try to show that African children have the same needs as children from other cultures. Such stories create the feeling of sameness, which is good; however, what they do not emphasize is our differences. These differences usually define the roles to which West Africans can aspire in a world culture that is marked by prejudice. If all children share the same fears and concerns, why do African children continue to be portrayed in rural settings, whereas White, Western children have the freedom to choose their world and activities? Western children are free to move between worlds, are free to reject one world in favor of another, and can even walk barefoot without being depicted as uncivilized.

Williams's *When Africa Was Home* (1991), set in South Africa, splendidly illustrates this point. Peter, the White hero, has to choose between an over-crowded modern city in the United States, and a sparse, underdeveloped rural community in Africa. He chooses the African village for its simplicity, but is fully aware that he can always leave his African playmates in their "natural" habitat and return to the modern city. Africa then becomes "home" for those White Westerners who want a change in lifestyle.

Exotic and Mysterious Culture

In *Flyaway Girl* (1992), Grifalconi captures a young girl's rite of passage from childhood into a responsible lifestyle as her mother awaits the coming of a new baby. Grifalconi depicts the exotic aspects of this experience as she creates a spooky background through her illustrations. According to Yulisa Amadu Maddy, a Sierra Leonean novelist who has taught in three African countries, Grifalconi "captures the African spirit, but the mistakes in the text confuse Western and Eastern Africa. The Masai of East Africa cannot be associated with the Benin mask that is shown in the illustrations" (quoted in MacCann & Richard, 1995, p. 42). Nonetheless, Grifalconi exploits these cultural artifacts to maximize the exotic appeal of the book.

Clifford's *Salah of Sierra Leone* (1975) tells the story of a youth who must do the right thing in the face of political upheavals in Sierra Leone. Clifford presents the indigenous Africans as corrupt and cruel in contrast to their political opponents, the Freetown Creoles, who are more capable of running the country. Through these Creoles, the Western superior ways are preferred over the African ways of doing things. Their familiarity with how the West does things legitimizes their position as the natural leaders of Sierra Leone, a country they were shipped back to when the British began having a conscience about slavery.

Clifford's main character, Salah, is an indigenous West African. His inferior status is contrasted from the beginning with his friend Luke's superior position in society. He is a Black African from "up country," while Luke is of mixed race, and from an elite Creole family. Salah lives in a local house, but his friend lives in a big colonial house on a hill. "The space and the number of rooms in this house astonished an up country boy who had grown up in a one-room thatch hut" (p. 9). When the story ends, Salah is made to do the "right" thing and betray his father's political party. Only civilized Creoles familiar with the Western ways of doing things should rule Sierra Leone, not his father's type—the "up country people in the bush" (p. 80).

These White authors find West African culture exotic and fascinating, but also wanting. West Africans are viewed as human beings with needs similar to those of the rest of the human race, but, unlike Westerners, they are uncivilized.

The Dominant Image of Nature and Romance

The dominant image of nature and romance maintains the power relationship that exists between Africa and the West. This image can reinforce the inferiority of Blackness that historically was constructed through slavery, imperialism, and colonialism (Du Bois, 1996; Irele, 1995), and can lead Black children in the West to reject the continent their ancestors once inhabited.

To White children in the West, this dominant image of Africa as natural and romantic can confirm their feelings of superiority and encourage them to rationalize the intervention in, and exploitation of, the African continent and its people. They may continue to invent "needs" for West Africans, "which goes hand in hand with the compulsion to help the needy, a noble and self-gratifying task that also renders the helper's service indispensable" (Minh-ha, 1995, p. 267). This subtle form of oppression continues to prevail among well-intentioned Westerners eager to assist developing countries whose differences they interpret as "awkwardness" or "incompleteness" (p. 264).

These cultural images are a concern because "what we see about ourselves often influences what we do about ourselves, [and] the role of image and the control of the mind is more important now in a media-saturated society than ever before in history" (Clarke, 1991, p. 329). Clarke goes on to say that "in an indirect way the image we accept of ourselves determines what we think of ourselves and what we do for ourselves" (p. 343). This seems to be a predicament for Africans in the modern world. Perhaps creating a dominant image of West Africa as natural and romantic is an easy way to escape the responsibility of addressing the complex nature of West Africa and West Africans—in a world that seeks to continue casting them as simple and dependent. On the other hand, perhaps it is all that the publishers are willing to produce as they target the Western audiences who have the purchasing power (Altbach, 1995; Khorana, 1994).

To Black authors, Africa continues to be home, a romantic place that is fondly remembered for its past glories and rich cultural practices. This ideology is embedded within the historical events that led to the forced migration of African Blacks now living in the diaspora. By refusing to acknowledge the existence of contemporary Africa, these authors are in a way depriving West Africa of its potential to evolve as a contemporary home for its current inhabitants.

Literature that insists on describing West Africa only in terms of its past accomplishments and ancient civilization ignores present-day West Africa, its complexities, and the challenges of modernization. Zipes (1993) interprets this persistence as social conditioning by the dominant ideology that inadvertently shapes the thinking of Blacks in the diaspora. Hanging on to an Africa that no longer exists, as a way of dealing with White, capitalistic oppression, serves the interest of White people in the sense that these Western Blacks may transmit the White, Western ideology of Western superiority that perpetuates African Blacks' inferiority status. By doing this they may also communicate a sense of their own superiority over other Blacks and may be oblivious to the subordinate position they occupy in the White, Western world that continues to serve as their home.

Complexity of Life in West Africa

Contemporary Africa is extremely complex. Neither completely traditional nor postcolonial (free from colonial domination) in practice, it continues to accommodate varied cultural practices. It is besieged by modern and traditional problems.

For example, Tutuola's *Ajaiyi and His Inherited Poverty* (1967) set in pre-colonial Nigeria, and Ekwensi's *The Drummer Boy* (1967/1988) set in post-colonial Nigeria explore the themes of poverty and survival. In Tutuola's novel, Ajaiyi raises money for his parents' funeral by pawning himself to a pawnbroker. After giving his parents a befitting burial, he works hard until his debts are paid. Life is not easy but he eventually makes it and returns home in better material condition. On the other hand, Akin, the hero in Ekwensi's *The Drummer Boy*, never really gets it as easy although he works hard too. Blind as he is, Akin tries to earn a living as a musician but is taken advantage of, robbed, and almost killed. Fortunately, he ends up in a reformatory school.

This seems to be a common experience in Lagos, Nigeria a postcolonial city, as well as in other postcolonial African cities such as Yaounde, Cameroon and Nairobi, Kenya. For example, in Mwangi's *Kill Me Quick* (1973), a novel set in contemporary Kenya, Meja, the protagonist, suffers as well. Despite the fact that he renders his services to a White plantation owner who employs him for a weekly wage, Meja is still unable to raise enough money to feed himself in Nairobi, a postcolonial city. He is exploited, but remains poor. He can smell the good life, but hard as he tries, he can never partake of it. Meja is sent to jail, returns home, and then flees back to the city to look for any job to assist his parents in raising his younger siblings. Meja is unable to explain to them the reality of the city and so he returns to his homeless state. These novels capture similar African youth experiences set in different time periods. They provide evidence that strategies that used to be effective in traditional Africa do not necessarily work in contemporary Africa.

To many White, Western authors, West African culture is "incomplete" (Minh-ha, 1995), but to many Black authors, the culture remains "pure" and untainted. Either way, West African identity remains to be defined in culturally authentic ways within children's literature.

Stereotypical Images and Projects of Possibility

Pointing out stereotypes and issues of authenticity in children's books does not mean I am advocating censorship. Instead, as a teacher, a mother, and a reader from West Africa who is socially responsible, I suggest critical literacy as one way in which teachers and parents can join others in projects of possibility (Simon, 1992; Peirce, 1992). Critical literacy demands that individuals from across cultures be socially responsible for the establishment of a just and equal society (Shannon, 1995). The ability to question signs and meanings embedded in texts empowers readers with skills that enable them to construct new knowledge by subverting these signs and the dominant messages they are expected to retrieve. Teaching children to "consciously subvert signs" (Myers, 1995, p. 582) enables them to read varying kinds of books in an empowering manner. Rather than accept these signs as absolute truths, children ask questions to uncover the different layers of meanings that are undergirded by specific ideologies.

Children should also realize that because society is complex, there is no formula for portraying life in Africa in texts. It then becomes each reader's social responsibility to negotiate personal meanings from existing texts, as well as other meanings that would make social change possible in our immediate and global communities.

Chapter Two
Illustrations and the Messages They Convey: African Culture in Picture Books

Writing and illustrating out of one's culture is a challenge, especially if the pictures included in the books communicate "misinformation" about the culture in question or perpetuate stereotypes. This has been and continues to be the plight of African culture depicted in children's books that are illustrated and/or written by those who hail from the West, and the United States in particular as I discussed in Chapter 1. One major reason why this problem has endured over the decades is because the big publishing houses "scurry" for literature that depicts human diversity. Unable to get "authentic" stories and pictures from Africans in Africa for various sociopolitical reasons, these publishers resort to using established illustrators/writers in the West (some of whom have lived in or visited different countries in Africa).

In this chapter I examine closely picture books about Africa illustrated by Leo and Diane Dillon, Ann Grifalconi, and Trina Schart Hyman. I chose these illustrators because they have all won major awards, have a vested interest in Africa, and three of them are listed in the top 100 most popular illustrators in America.[1] Grifalconi, who did not make the list, however, has written and/or illustrated over fifty books.[2] These illustrators therefore are not only experienced professionals, but are highly regarded in the publishing industry.

Although all four have published extensively, this chapter will focus on nine of their picture books. These picture books, published between 1975 and 2002 and spanning almost a thirty-year period, are indicators of how much their illustrations have evolved over the years to reflect the dynamism of African cultures and what messages these illustrators communicate about Africa. As Ellen Handler Spitz (1999) notes, "[e]ven when they are not intended to do so, picture books provide children with some of their earliest takes on morality, taste, and basic cultural knowledge, including messages about gender, race, and class" (p. 14). A major part of my discussion will dwell on the subtle ways these illustrators' cultural backgrounds may have inadvertently affected the messages they paint in their pictures.

In the introductory chapter of Critical Perspectives on Postcolonial African Children's and Young Adult Literature (1998), Meena Khorana posed the following question: "Are African children continuing to be colonized through the literature being written and produced for them?" (p. 2). Donnarae MacCann and Yulisa Amadu Maddy also echo this sentiment. These and other Africanist scholars of children's literature (myself included) are aware of the fact that portraying Africa in children's books will always remain a challenge. One major reason is because of our colonial heritage. Another reason is because of the nature of the publishing business. However, we also know that it is our social responsibility to draw readers' attention to stereotypes and cultural inaccuracies that may be prevalent in such books.

The question of an author/illustrator's identity is not new, however, and I do not want to dwell too much on it here. According to Trinh Minh-ha, identity arguments encourage "binary opposites," a concept which she finds defeating if we want to heal whole communities. In Woman, Native, Other: Writing Post-coloniality and Feminism (1989), she remarks: "Despite our desperate eternal attempt to separate, contain, mend, categories always leak" (p. 94). Her skepticism notwithstanding, it is still necessary for scholars to not only read books and pictures carefully, to check for factual omissions, cultural misrepresentations, and stereotypes, but to also see how some of these errors or problems are a result of one's cultural identity.[3] In other words, it is necessary to understand how one's position as an "other" can taint the messages embedded in the pictures one depicts. It also helps us to understand that illustrations "establish settings . . . reinforce text . . . extend or develop the plot, [and] establish mood" (Jacobs and Tunnell, 2004, p. 37).

The research question guiding my analysis in this chapter is simply: How do award-winning illustrators from the West portray life in Africa? After carefully reading through the print and visual texts of the nine books included in this study, I identified four messages. These are: Africa as a "Mythical Home" with unexplainable natural and historical occurrences; Africa as a vulnerable place prone to foreign invasions; Africa as a place where people share space with animals; and Africans as dignified people with varied cultures.

Africa as a "Mythical Home" with Unexplainable Natural and Historical Occurrences

Two books, The Village of Round and Square Houses and The Village that Vanished, written and/or illustrated by Ann Grifalconi depict this image. This means that for over sixteen years (from 1986 to 2002) her perception of Africa did not change. She continues to prefer the village as a setting, and as

Raoul Granqvist (1997) notes, she uses "Africa as a site of Arcadian recollections" (p. 28).

In her award-winning picture book, *The Village of Round and Square Houses*, Grifalconi explains why women and men live in two kinds of houses in Tos, a village in Cameroon. It is a fascinating story narrated by a female character. However, as can be predicted, it highlights the exotic nature of the Tos culture Grifalconi is writing about. As though she is afraid that some readers may question the credibility of her story, she adds:

> This village really exists—just the way it always has—in the remote hills of the Cameroons in Central Africa. It is almost entirely isolated, with no paved roads close to it than a full eight hours away. None but the most adventurous visitor would dare risk the steep and bumpy, rocky clay paths leading to the thatch-roofed village that clings to the side of an almost extinct volcano. (unpaged)

As Grifalconi explains, she risked her life not only to capture this exotic cultural tradition, but also to listen to the horrifying tale behind the practice. Her illustrations—representational art—verify the print text. She captures the people with dignity and respect using soft earth colors to add contrast to the images, although some of the exotic images look scary. For her effort, she was rewarded with a Caldecott honor in 1987.

The first picture the reader sees is of the narrator, a young girl dressed in purple garment, with large, round earrings dangling from her ears, and bangles on her wrist. She is lying between a round and a square house on a moonlit night. She has a mischievous smile on her face, which adds to the mystery of the "mythical" story narrated in the book. The subsequent pictures show family life and other daily activities among the Tos people as the narrator explains why they have such an unconventional living arrangement. One can tell that the inhabitants have learned to co-exist with nature, in particular with Naka mountain—"old mother Naka" who smokes "peacefully" like Gran'ma Tika (unpaged).

However, it wasn't always so, for a long time ago the mountain had actually erupted, frightening the villagers who had

> cried out to Naka
> And prayed where they were lying down,
> Hands pressing the earth asking:
> What have we done to anger you? (unpaged)

When the volcanic eruption finally ended, "Everything was covered with ash . . . Everyone looked like a gray ghost" (unpaged). The important thing, however, was that "NAKA HAD SPARED THEM!" (unpaged).

The visual images evoke warmth, humility, and a sense of mystery as the villagers acknowledge the superior power of nature. The images communicate the notion of Africa as a "mythical home," a term used by Raoul Granqvist (1997, p. 24). There is a good contrast in color between Tos of the past and that of the present; purple and other bright colors are interspersed with orange and gray to establish the vibrancy of the community and the myth that continues to haunt them.

Grifalconi's *The Village that Vanished*, a Jane Addams Honor book, although not illustrated by her, also reinforces the exotic and mythical themes that run through most of her picture books set in Africa. The detailed illustrations on the jacket cover capture an air of mystery. The contrast between the thriving green forest and the orange sky with silhouettes of soldiers prepares the reader for the conflict that lies ahead. Abikanile (one of three protagonists), in a beautiful outfit and with a pot on her head, stands with poise and gazes at the horizon. She understands there is trouble ahead but does not know what kind.

Using an African storytelling technique, Grifalconi introduces the story by highlighting the Yao people's belief in ancestors and the supernatural, especially in times of trouble. Abikanile's mother, Njemile, invokes the spirits of their ancestors, using words that foreshadow later events in the story.

> Oh, my ancestor spirits!
> Oh, my grandmothers,
> Oh, my father, sister spirits!
> Hear me now in our need!
>
> I hear your ancestor voices
> Singing in the grass, the trees,
> In the winds, the waters . . .
> I need your magic
> Do not deny me now!
> Lend me and my children
> The secrecy of the crocodile
> Below your waters!
>
> Oh, my ancestor spirits,
> We need your magic now!
> Protect our village
> Keep us free! (unpaged)

Nelson's illustrations extend the text and intensify this air of mystery in the next double-page spread and in subsequent pictures. Abikanile can now tell the kind of trouble the village is facing: "The slavers were coming!" (unpaged). Although she does not understand why "violent men from the north" would "want to sell [their] labor . . . to foreign masters," she knows that she can count on Njemile, the people of her village, her grandmother, Chimwala, and their ancestors. Grifalconi gives these women a sense of agency, as together with the old men and children they make their village disappear, leaving only Chimwala's hut standing. To be consistent with the theme of mystery surrounding the Yao people, Chimwala (meaning "stone") is portrayed as fearless, wise, and mythical. She is as "silent as a stone . . . [and] as calm as a stone" (unpaged), echoing the "stone path" the ancestors later reveal to Abikanile.

Grifalconi's use of the stone metaphor to explain the combined strength of the grandmother, the granddaughter, and the ancestral spirits is compelling. She emphasizes the belief or lack thereof in ancestors, and its consequences. Ancestral worship, which some consider as magic in this book, again reinforces the mythical theme that pervades the entire setting, characters, and mood of the story, with lines repeated to emphasize the mysteriousness of the experience. Thus it communicates on different levels that Africans need their ancestors to survive in their environment.

Because the text lacks specific historical details regarding the slave trade being depicted, the illustrations also suffer. Brenda Randolph (2003) draws readers' attention to this when she remarks that depicting "only Black slavers . . . in the illustrations [can be] troubling for some" (p. 66). It is particularly troubling because Njemile actually explains to her daughter that "Our people are put in chains and sold into slavery to foreign masters!" (unpaged). However, it is not quite clear who the masters are. Also, the African slave "trackers" have facial expressions that make them appear more vicious than their Arab leaders.

Some reviewers have raised other important questions about this book.[4] For example: What specific slave trade is the author trying to depict—the Atlantic or the Sahara? Because Grifalconi sets her story in an historical past, factual accuracy becomes a major issue that makes one wonder about the political ideology behind her depiction of the event. Using this lens to interpret the story text and illustrations, as Peter Hollindale (1992), Jack Zipes (1993), and Raoul Granqvist (1997) contend, makes it possible not only to identify overt meanings in the text but also to look for covert messages Grifalconi may be communicating about slavery and Africans. For instance, by focusing on a generic slave trade, is she implying that only Arabs and Africans were involved in this horrific practice? If so, then it means that she wants to absolve Europeans and Whites for the major role they played during the transatlantic slave trade. As Granqvist (1997) postulates, authors and illustrators must be very careful about "a second [and] less overt [message] which readers have to look for in the literary organization of the text rather than in inherent guidelines" (p. 24).

The information Grifalconi presents about the Yao people is also murky. She is mainly concerned with showing how the Yao people use ancestral worship and the supernatural to save themselves from ruthless slavers. Thus they remain a group of Africans who have mysterious ways to deal with unexplainable occurrences in their village. This obsession inadvertently compromises her work and in a way shapes the illustrator's visual interpretation of the text as he confirms her message without necessarily using pictures as a means to fill in the obvious gaps in the tale.

Africa as a Vulnerable Place Prone to Foreign Invasions

Closely related to the "mythical home" image is the notion of Africa as a vulnerable place that is easily invaded by outsiders/foreigners. The two books discussed in this category have both been illustrated by Leo and Diane Dillon: Khephra Burns's *Mansa Musa: A Lion in Mali* (2001), a fictionalized biography of Mali's fourteenth-century king, and Leontyne Price's *Aida* (1990). While the illustrations are attractive and well executed, I believe that illustrating texts laden with inaccurate historical facts can be burdensome and tricky, especially since the Dillons have limited experience with "historical illustrations . . . for picture books.[5] Thus, as beautiful as the illustrations are, this lack of consistency in historical details in the texts can compromise an artist's work. Did Khephra Burns do justice to the subject; and how well did Dillon and Dillon's interpretation stay faithful to the text, capturing cultural and historical details, or extending and filling gaps in the story? I was disappointed by all the negative reviews[6] regarding the historical content of the story and wondered why the Dillons had wasted their talent and effort on the book.

Mansa Musa: A Lion in Mali is the story of a young boy who was captured and sold into slavery, but later became one of the greatest kings in fourteenth-century Mali. According to Stephen Belcher (2002), "young readers may enjoy the (very predictable) story, and the book itself is very well produced with extensive illustrations by Leo and Diane Dillon" (p. 4). However, he also notes that some illustrations tend to blend cultures. For example, "one illustration shows the initiant Musa in an Egyptian temple or tomb, whose walls are decorated with relief carvings of Mande Komo masks (the Komo is an initiatory society) and Dogon dance masks" (p. 4). The illustrations in the book are a series of tableaux showcasing the Malian people, their culture, and their historical struggles with outside invaders within a particular period that has defined present-day Mali. The book reflects this image as it echoes the theme of ancestral worship that makes Africans at times vulnerable to ruthless foreigners who take advantage of our hospitality. Burns remarks in the prologue:

> It was a source of great pride to the whole village to be admired by outsiders. If a stranger appeared in their midst, they put a festive display of music and dance and lavished gifts upon the visitor so that he might later boast of Mali's greatness in his travels. Besides, a number of the elders were members of the Keita clan that, according to tradition, was descended from a wanderer from the east. One never knew if such a stranger might not be the spirit of a returning ancestor. (unpaged)

Thus, unlike in Grifalconi's *The Village That Vanished*, the stranger here is welcomed; however, like the strangers in Grifalconi's book he disrupts the community. Although this book has been criticized for historical inaccuracies, at least the specific slave trade is identified. Parker (1996) also notes that the Dillons's "illustrations leave the reader or viewer with a sense of mystery and appreciation which can be shared by young and old. They also create images that complement and enhance the author's intent" (p. 4). This means that depiction of cultural inaccuracies may be a result of a faulty text.

Leontyne Price's *Aida* is another book that represents the image of Africa as vulnerable to outside invasions. Based on an opera, *Aida* tells the story of an Ethiopian princess's experience as a daughter, slave, and lover. She is captured by the Egyptians who make her a slave and subsequently she falls in love with the "enemy," her captor. It is a beautiful story of romance and treachery that can be touching at times. Dillon and Dillon bring the story to life through their illustrations. As in *Mansa Musa*, the exquisite illustrations are a series of tableaux with borders that further interpret the events in the story. Parker (1996) adds that "the Dillons have adorned each page of the story with elaborate decoration and ornamentation. Beautifully illustrated, the story is a fascinating array in full color palette of design and draftsmanship" (p. 4).

The Dillons consistently place a picture of one set of characters as borders of the verso pages and a full-length picture of the key characters on the opposite page, as they reinforce the text of this tragic story. In so doing, readers are able to guess the characters' social status based on their clothing and the way the illustrators position them vis-à-vis one another on the different pages. This book, which was cited for the 1991 Coretta Scott King Award, is one of the Dillons's favorites (see McElmeel, 2000, p. 147). The entire story focuses on Aida surviving in captivity; hence the image of Africa vulnerable to foreign invasions is taken to a different level. Not only do Africans not have control over their physical (geographical) space, but they do not necessarily have much control over their emotional and spiritual states as well. Thus they are susceptible to all kinds of invasions from outsiders who may not mean them well.

Africa as a Place Where People Share Space with Animals

Discussing two views about the role of art in society, Ellen Handler Spitz (1999) remarks that "although art surely *does* offer an alternative realm of imaginary experience, it also produces a direct emotional experience" (p. 208). In her analysis of a number of picture books, Spitz explains that fear is psychological and that darkness creates a situation through which children can master this fear (pp. 24–36). Perhaps this is what Grifalconi is trying to accomplish in *Darkness and the Butterfly*. Although the book lacks an engaging storyline, the illustrations amplify the exotic themes Grifalconi associates with Africans through the young female character's fear of darkness. The first thing a reader notices on the cover and the front pages is the jungle setting. Osa, surrounded by scary animals, pokes her head through the blank white space near the middle of the page. The story text then follows:

> Have you ever been afraid of the dark?
> Of being alone in the night
> When strange things float by
> That seem to follow you . . .
> With eyes that glow in the darkness? (unpaged)

At this point it becomes clear that Grifalconi is simply showcasing exotic animals that exist in the village of Tos. Her pictures remain beautiful, but the jungle we first see is depicted in blue, pink, read, green, orange, and purple colors with different animals in different shades of these colors. This may be her way of showing how baseless this fear is, as she tells the story of how Osa overcame her fear of darkness. The heroine succeeds in conquering her fear with the help of a wise woman who confirms that

> When I was alone I used to get scared, too—
> specially at night! [because]
> darkness hides everything. (unpaged)

If Osa would only follow the "yellow butterfly," she would overcome her fear too. The little girl follows her advice, and when she finally overcomes this fear of darkness, the animals no longer look as threatening. They are no longer depicted in fancy colors but are now in their natural earth-tone colors. Osa realizes that animals will remain a major part of her world and that she need not fear that they will harm her; rather, she must learn to co-exist with them in the same space. The underlying message here is that Africans are no different from the domestic and wild animals with which they share space. It would be stupid then to be afraid of any animal!

Ethnic Notions: Black People in White Minds (1987), a powerful documentary about the Black experience in America, also addresses the issue of White people's obsession with linking Blacks and animals. Consequently, it becomes hard not to feel uneasy with illustrators who perpetuate this message. While it is true that one can find animals in residential areas in most African countries, especially in rural areas, these are domestic animals for the most part. It will therefore help if Western illustrators include animals in their books about Africa in a realistic manner without necessarily sending messages that may be construed as White superiority. Although simple, *Darkness and the Butterfly* is an entertaining story. If a reader can go beyond the obvious miscommunications about Africans and their relationships with jungle animals, he or she can identify the universal theme of fear of the dark and may realize that although "darkness may envelop the world, . . . love and self endure" (Spitz, 1999, p. 34).

Trina Schart Hyman is another illustrator who seems obsessed with the image of Africans living with animals. Her pictorial depiction of Cameroon in *Sense Pass King*, written by her daughter, Katrin Hyman Tchana, demonstrates this. This is a charming story about a young girl who consistently outsmarts the king and eventually earns the people's respect in the community. According to Leslie Moore, it

> demonstrates the type of power people exercised in many African societies in precolonial times. Unworthy leaders often found themselves without a community to lead when the people switched their allegiance to a leader perceived as more just and capable. (quoted in Randolph, 2003, p. 66)

Indeed, it is an engaging heroic tale with splendid illustrations that extend the text. However, as always, Hyman adds too many animals in the setting. One wonders at times why a particular animal is in the company of humans.

It is disappointing that Hyman insists on looking at Cameroonians, regardless of where the story takes place, through the same lens. For instance, despite some cultural overlaps, there are significant differences between the northwest region of Cameroon, where *Sense Pass King* is set, and the northern region, where *The Fortune-Tellers*, by Lloyd Alexander (1992), takes place. However, this is not reflected in the choice of animals Hyman includes in her illustrations for these books. Similarly, in *Sense Pass King* Tchana's (2002) text states: "When she was three, she [Sense Pass King] could prepare dinner for her parents" (unpaged). Hyman illustrates this scene with pictures of Sense Pass King walking across a big yard with a tray of food; right next to her are roosters, lizards, a chick, and three big cockroaches. Because the author does not mention the specific animals that accompany Sense Pass King, Hyman presents the animals she believes are representative of this region. The greatest strength of this book, however, is its sense of adventure and the agency Tchana ascribes to her lead character. I find this empowering because most of us grew up listening to the original folk tale in which a male character always outwits the king.

Leo and Diane Dillon's illustrations for *Why Mosquitoes Buzz in People's Ears*, text by Verna Aardema (1975), has a different twist to the role humans and animals play in their shared environment. As is typical of pourquoi tales, whereby authors explain a specific natural phenomenon or custom within a particular region, *Why Mosquitoes Buzz in People's Ears* explains this phenomenon simply. Both the story and the illustrations, done in collage, capture this world brilliantly. With the forest as the designated setting, the Dillons painstakingly illustrate images of each creature mentioned and more, as they interpret the tale visually for their young readers. Thus affinity with animals is contextualized, because the reader meets the only human being in the story on the last page, slapping the noisy mosquito dead. The African's relationship with the forest animals is clear. Although set in a generic West Africa, the Dillons capture the activities in the forest splendidly, demonstrating what

Mabel Segun (1997), an African writer/illustrator of children's books, describes as maintaining the "harmony" in picture books. By this she means there are no incongruities among the text, illustrations, and the culture being depicted that would confuse the reader (p. 97). The African farmer is not really part of the forest world; however, he co-exists with the forest creatures and shares their dislike for mosquitoes that are constantly "whining in people's ears" or telling nonsensical stories, as the Iguana has long concluded (unpaged).

Sharron McElmeel (2000) observes that the Dillons "often use their illustrations to create visual subplots in the books they illustrate. In *Why Mosquitoes Buzz in People's Ears* they put a little red bird in each. The bird witnesses the story as it unfolds" (p. 149). Unlike Hyman's juxtaposition of Africans and animals, there is a logical reason behind the relationship in the Dillons's illustration, which does not keep the reader wondering why the lone African is there. Indeed, Dillon and Dillon do a wonderful job in all their books including this pourqoui tale, which earned them a much-deserved Caldecott award.

Africans as Dignified People with Varied Cultures

The only book identified under this category is Margaret Musgrove's *Ashanti to Zulu: African Traditions*, illustrated by the Dillons. Their visual depiction of African culture in this book is impressive and helped to establish who Africans are to their Western audience. According to Barbara Bader (2002), "by the end of the 1970s an image of African beauty—Ashanti to Zulu or Masai—was as fixed in the minds of many American youngsters as the Greek or Europeans" (p. 671). That is how powerful the Dillons's illustrations are!

Ashanti to Zulu: African Traditions is an alphabet book that painstakingly displays twenty-six different cultures in Africa. Thus it debunks the myth of Africa as one country and of Africans as one people. The Dillons capture each culture in a picture frame creating a breathtaking photo album. As Parker (1996) rightly observes, this seems to be a "noticeable and distinctive aspect of their style" (p. 4). The Dillons also appear to be making a conscious effort in this book to depict whole communities across continental Africa. Thus it is no surprise that they "include a man, a woman, a child, their living quarters, an artifact, and an animal generally found in that area of Africa" (McElmeel, 2000, p. 148). The last framed picture is that of a map of Africa. On this the Dillons identify the twenty-six cultures paraded in the alphabet book. Although they focus more on ancient civilization and rural communities, as Musgrove's text stipulates, they have done justice to the experience.

For Barbara Bader (1998), only one word can describe their artwork. "That word is arresting, and it will almost invariably do. They are intrinsically designers, not illustrators. Their elaborate, highly polished artwork can obscure a simple story" (p. 146). Lawrance M. Bernabo (2002), a professor of Cultural Studies at Lake Superior College and a top reviewer for Amazon.com, shares this sentiment. He notes, however, that in *Ashanti to Zulu*, "there's admittedly a degree of artificiality to some of these compositions"(unpaged). Regardless, it is hard to find many educators who would not be taken by the illustrations in this book. For their effort, the Dillons received another Caldecott medal in 1977.

Illustrators and Their Messages about Africa: What Accounts for These Images?

The answer to this question may seem obvious to many; however, when one pauses to reflect, it is not really quite simple. It is becoming harder to determine who can accurately depict African cultural experiences. According to Khorana, colonialism continues as a factor in the production of books for children. This means that some African illustrators may not have completely transcended their colonized state. In this case vestiges of colonialism may continue to affect their visual interpretations of Africans and their culture. This seems to be exactly what Trinh Minh-ha may be referring to when she states that "the search for an identity is, therefore usually a search for that lost, pure, true, real, genuine, original, authentic self, often situated within a process of elimination of all that is considered other, superfluous, fake, corrupted, or Westernized" ("Not You/ Like You: Post-colonial Women," 1998). And, of course, it is hard to be an "original African" illustrator when our entire continent continues to be besieged by Western values. Segun (1997) observes, however, that professional training is the key. According to her, artists with little or no training, regardless of how much they know about the culture or how well they are immersed in it, cannot capture the images well (p. 77). Flora Nwapa (1997) adds that money is a motivating factor. She remarks that in her professional experience as an author and publisher of children's books in Nigeria, the few African artists who can illustrate books well are unwilling to experiment or go beyond. They see illustrating for children simply as a job, and do not feel the need to make sacrifices because of the negligible financial reward (pp. 269–270).

This, therefore, leaves the task primarily with Western illustrators. Training is not the issue for this group of professionals. What we should really worry about is their attitude, their willingness to do extensive research, and their sense of empathy. African scholars must remain alert because some of these Western illustrators, like their African peers, do not live in a vacuum. They are part of our global society that has a long history of oppression, exclusion, and cultural supremacy and, if they are not careful, they may end up painting messages of White Western superiority in their picture books about Africa.

Why is it that Grifalconi and Hyman, who have visited Africa and, in Hyman's case, even has Cameroonian relatives, insist on the exotic and mythical experiences of Africans, whereas Dillon and Dillon, who have never traveled to Africa, are able to capture a variety of images? Perhaps it has something to do with the fact that the Dillons had decided earlier in their career that they "wanted to represent all races and to show people that were rarely seen in children's books" (Leo Dillon's Interview + Transcript, 2004, at scholatic.com). With such a lofty goal, they have worked extremely hard to capture our shared humanity without compromising the cultural differences that define us as collective groups of people within a particular region, and as individuals with specific stories to tell. the inside cover of The Village of Round and Square Houses (1986) states that Grifalconi "has had a long-standing interest in African peoples and cultures" (unpaged). By "interest," does she mean Africans as interesting subjects or objects to be talked about from a distance? Although she seems to enjoy the subjects she writes about and illustrates, somehow over the decades she has been unable to represent/perceive her African subjects as equals. They remain exotic and share nothing with her. Hyman's experience with Africans or Blacks as subjects of her illustrations is quite recent. Perhaps her struggle lies in the fact that even though she has an African family now, she remains a stranger to this new culture which she still does not fully understand. She never transcends her touristic images of animals scattered all over northern and northwestern Cameroon, which she may have noticed when she visited the country.

Everyone has a right to set his/her stories anywhere; however, authors should be socially responsible, even though some editors and publishers of children's books may feel otherwise.[7] Echoing Jacqueline Woodson's (1998) sentiments, I believe it is important for each one of these illustrators to ask themselves candidly what exactly they are bringing to the African experience; what is it that they "have to offer and/or say about it?" (p. 37). Doing this will help each to examine what Woodson acknowledges as "one's position of power" vis-à-vis the African subject of their illustrations.

All four illustrators discussed above must be commended for attempting to depict Africa in picture books. However, I hope that they will continue to illustrate books for children from diverse cultural backgrounds with greater awareness in order to avoid falling into the trap of perpetuating unflattering or false images. I also hope that as Western authors and illustrators try their best to represent Africa's humanity, Africans should not just sit on the fence and wait for them to fail or make grievous mistakes that will continue to create tension. Those with talent and enough motivation should seek proper training as Segun recommends. They should also experiment with their art a lot more as they learn to "depict African features with grace" (Mhlophe, 2003, p. 11). They should realize that "art is both safe and unsafe," and our engagement in "the task of cultural transmission . . . never ends. [It is a] task that we must not put off" (Spitz, 1999, p. 215). It is in this vein that I continue to examine critically the images of Africa in children's books.

Chapter Three
The "Typical" West African Village Stories

> I had dreamed of seeing Africa from the time I was a child. It was the wild animals roaming through jungles and grasslands that I fell in love with first and wanted to see up close. As I grew older; I realized that Africa was far more than a home for elephants and lions, but I still yearned to go there . . . Our plan was to follow a route that would avoid the major cities. There are heavily populated urban and industrial areas in Africa, but we wanted to concentrate on the more remote parts of the continents. Our goals were to witness the natural beauty of the land and learn something of the culture and customs of its people. (Scott, 1993, p. 7)

This quotation captures the fate of Africa and Africans when viewed through Western eyes. In this chapter, I will carry on the dialogue on image making as I examine other genres of children's literature. Although Africa is one of the most geographically and socially diverse continents in the world, when most Westerners consider Africa they tend to think of animals and primitive villages. While animals and villages are certainly still part of African reality, so are large metropolitan areas, factories, and modern forms of transportation. What keeps the image of Africa in the past and what consequences does such an image have for Africans?

Africa is a large continent—much larger in comparison to other continents than is typically depicted on Western maps—with over 52 nations and thousands of ethnic groups and languages. The diversity is such that many representations of Africa are possible. We can think of bankers in Cape Town, open market vendors in Cairo, herders in Nandi, farmers in Banso, or bus drivers in Algiers. Such diversity makes it unlikely that any one person, even an African, could capture the authentic African experience because there is not one experience that can be labeled African.

Yet when it comes to representations of Africa in children's books, one image prevails. The diversity of Africa is reduced to a particular version of its past. By looking at literature from English-speaking West Africa geared toward children in grades K through 3, I hope to demonstrate further the narrow vision of Africa in the works of children's authors. My analysis will provide a rationale for why Scott knew that Africa was more than jungles and grassland, but wanted only to see the idyllic settings and primitive cultures when he arrived.

I analyzed thirty books altogether—folklore, illustrated stories, and picture books of early childhood. The oldest book in the group was written in 1947, and the most recent, a collection of folktales, was written in 2002. Six of these books were written by Africans.

Folklore

All eleven collections or picture book versions of folklore have village or jungle settings. Like such literature from other parts of the world, West African folklore describes worthy virtue. Because it is often expected to keep the customs of an area in our memories, perhaps it is understandable that West African folklore is set in the past, always in villages. Unfortunately, the books seem to define the past, complete with a half-naked storyteller that tells stories, "through smoke of a village fire, with the dark forest trees as background and to the accompaniment of chirping crickets, the croaking of frogs in the stream, and the distant call of the jackal and hyena" (*The Magic Drum*, Burton, 1961, p. 15).

Courlander and Herzog's collection of folktales is the oldest (1947). They consciously ignore African development. In the preface to *The Cow-Tail Switch and Other West African Stories*, they note, "there are many country people and townspeople, tiny villages and great cities," but "here come some of the stories of the people of the forests, the seacoast, the hills and the plains." Where are stories of the great cities?

Walker's *The Dancing Palm Tree and Other Nigerian Folktales* (1990), like Haskett's *Some Gold, A Little Ivory* (1971) are set in the village/jungle. Walker explains to her Western audience:

> You will find that the truths taught in the stories prevail not only in Nigeria but all around the world, truths that people must learn to live by no matter what country they call home . . . And through these tales, it is hoped, we shall all become better acquainted with our brothers in West Africa. (p. 13)

Walker sees her collection of folklore as a bridge toward understanding the African cultural experience. She calms her audience by showing that West African villagers learn the Western universal moral truths on how to be human, even if they must live in the jungle and share living space with animals. Don't worry, she implies, Africans are humans too.

The jungle serves as a splendid setting for the Anansi stories that are a hallmark of West African literature. McDermott's *Anansi, the Spider* (1972), Kimmel's

Anansi Goes Fishing (1992) and *Anansi and the Moss-Covered Rock* (1988) are prime examples of this representation of West African tradition. Although the Anansi tales are about wit and vanity, McDermott dwells on the rural setting, "this story is from a long established culture, the Ashanti of West Africa, in the country of Ghana. Ghana is a green stronghold of dense rainforests between the ocean and the desert" (preface). Unlike McDermott and Kimmel, Arkhurst uses human beings as main characters in her recreations of Anansi tales in *The Adventure of the Spider* (1964), yet she retains the jungle settings. Apparently, there aren't any spiders in the cities of Ghana. Gail Haley's main character is also a human being. Her *A Story, A Story* (1970), a Caldecott winner, explains how Ananse, the Spider man brought stories to his people. Another popular tale that is set in Ghana is Angela Shelf Medearis' *Too Much Talk* (1995). It is a humorous story about a group of people who abandoned their village because familiar objects could speak.

In his recent collection *Favorite African Folktales* that won the NAACP award, Nelson Mandela (2002) shares some popular stories from across the continent. Two that are set in West Africa, "The Snake Chief" and "Spider and the Crow" explore the Rumpelstilskin and Anansi motifs.

Pourquoi Tales

There are many pourquoi tales among children's literature about West Africa. Perhaps the most famous author of such tales in North America is Verna Aardema, who wrote *Anansi Finds a Fool* (1992), *Why Mosquitoes Buzz in People's Ears* (1975), *Tales of the Third Ear* (1969), and *The Na of Wa* (1960). Her tales are all set in jungles or villages.

Gerson's *Why the Sky is Far Away* (1992) like Aardema's is also set in a village. It is a picture book, which uses expressionistic illustrations to depict primitive people who live as subsistence farmers because of excessive greed. Dayrell's *Why The Sun and The Moon Live in the Sky* (1968), also set in Nigeria, focuses on the friendship between the sun and the moon. Blair Lent's beautiful folk art illustrations place the story in a village. The originality and uniqueness of the illustrations earned him a Caldecott honor award. Anderson's *The Origin of Life on Earth* (1991) gives a Yoruba traditional version of the origin of humans where a black god with golden chains creates life. In similar ways, Lester's *How Many Spots Does a Leopard Have* (1989), Bryan's *Beat the Story Drum, Pum Pum* (1980), Dayrell's *Why the Sun and Moon Live in the Sky* (1968), and Green's *Folktales and Fairy Tales* (1967) represent Africans as primitive jungle or village dwellers. A slight variation is found in Achebe and Iroaganachi's *How the Leopard Got Its Claws* (1972). Although Achebe and Iroaganachi select a jungle setting, a reader can easily infer from the events that they do capture the political chaos of the times of decolonization of West Africa.

Books of Early Childhood

This category is a bit of a catchall for this study: two alphabet books, three counting books, and two poetry books. Ifeoma Onyefulu, an African author, uses photographs to portray an authentic African village setting in *A is for Africa* (1993). She notes, "This alphabet is based on my favorite images of the Africa I know . . . I wanted to capture what the people of Africa have in common: traditional life, warm family ties, and above all, the hospitality for which Africans are famous" (preface). In this book, Onyefulu exposes the reader to different objects, activities, and artifacts prevalent among the Igbos as she teaches children letters of the alphabet.

Although her photographs are beautiful, they show that even insiders seem to see Africa only in the past or through one lens. Onyefulu, an African residing in Europe and writing primarily for Western audiences, seems willing to represent Africa as one big village and through Western eyes. A second alphabet book, also titled *A is for Africa* (Owoo, 1992) presents modern Africa. Owoo shows us children going to school, using computers, and adults as fishermen, carpenters, political activists, and farmers. People are hard at work, fully clothed, and interested in change. In this book, Westerners get a glimpse of what it's like to be in West Africa in the 1990s.

Most counting books about Africa are usually set in the village or the jungle as well. As with the folk literature already discussed above, they do have their merits. However, unlike folk literature, counting books lend themselves to a more diverse setting. I will begin with Onyefulu's *Emeka's Gift* (1995). As usual her photographs of the villagers are interesting but predictable. Ruby Dee's *Two Ways to Count to Ten* (1988) offers well-written texts and beautiful illustrations about African life in the jungle. Hartmann's *One Sun Rises* (1994) focuses on the "African wildlife" (unpaged). All in all, these authors tend to romanticize the African village or past where/when life is/was considered simpler. Onyefulu (1993) claims warmth and hospitality.

Besides counting books, poetry books for young children set in Africa also celebrate the village. While Olaleye's *The Distant Talking Drum* (1995), a beautiful collection of poetry, glorifies the simplicity of Nigerian village life, Virginia Kroll's *Jaha and Jamil Went Down the Hill* (1995) emphasizes the exotic aspects of African culture. Uzo Unobagha's *Off to the Sweet Shores of Africa* (2000), however, blends the two; she does not merely celebrate her Nigerian village culture, but insinuates that sharing space with exotic animals is normal.

Before proceeding with the discussion in this chapter I must return briefly to one particular folktale: Wilson's *The Great Minu* (1974). *The Great Minu*, which I have deliberately placed last, illustrates the belief that Africans do and should prefer village life over city life. It's a humorous story about a simple farmer who leaves the farm to seek his fortune in the city. Because of the different ways of the city, he is confused about how to act and what to say. Each attempt to communicate with city folk is met with the response "minu," which means,

"I do not understand." When the farmer inquires about the name of the deceased in a passing funeral, he receives the reply, minu. To which he responds:

Mr. Minu is dead? Wailed the farmer. Poor Mr. Minu? So he had to leave all his wealth—his herd of cows, his buildings, his grand hotel and his fine shop—and die, die just like a poor person. Well, well in the future I'll be content to live a simple life, to breathe the fresh air on my little farm, and to help the poor people in my village. (p. 30)

This nostalgia for the simple life always seems to come from authors who have experienced and often succeeded in modern society. They feel their lives burdened with the demands of the present and look back blindly to a myth when times were "simpler," "more hospitable," and "sincere." Failing to remember those times within their own countries, Westerners turn their focus on simpler people—the stereotypical Africans. What seems to be forgotten in their accounts is the difficulty of simple village life, the hardships that pervade this lifestyle.

While it may seem to be progress that I could easily find 30 children's books concerned with West Africa, I think we must be careful with the messages that this increased attention brings. Nearly all the books (K–3) reviewed represented West Africa as a jungle dotted with occasional primitive villages. No one seems to work in these villages. This view of Africa positions Africans as uncomplicated beings who possess some supernatural affinity for animals but little ingenuity or desire. Although Africa possesses an abundance of natural resources, Africans seem incapable of harnessing them in any way that might bring them into the twenty-first century.

These books do not present an accurate picture of the complexities and diversities of the continent, even of one "chamber" of Africa (Appiah, 1992). bell hooks offers a way to think about why the representation is so standard across so many books when she discusses her experience in the United States.

Without a way to name our pain, we are also without words to articulate our pleasure. Indeed, a fundamental task of black critical thinkers has been the struggle to break with the hegemonic modes of seeing, thinking and being that block our capacity to see ourselves oppositionally, to imagine, describe and invent ourselves in ways that are liberatory. Without this, how can we challenge and invite non-black allies and friends to dare to look at us differently, to dare to break their colonizing gaze? (hooks, 1992, p. 2)

hooks suggests the insiders' capability in the continuation of Westerners' colonial gaze at Africa. This insider/outsider issue is a continuing debate over whether books written by outsiders can represent Africa at all accurately and whether such books should be allowed in schools. For example, scholars and educators have questioned the racist content of such "classics" as Kipling's jungle stories, Burnett's *The Secret Garden,* or Conrad's *Heart of Darkness.* During an interview, Achebe states, "it's not in my nature to talk about banning books . . . I'm saying, read it with the kind of understanding and with the knowledge I talk about. And read it beside African works" (Winkler, 1994, p. 9). Yet, these children's books are dominated by a colonial gaze regardless of whether outsiders or insiders wrote them. Until more authors represent African diversity and the dynamic nature of all African cultures, Achebe's side-by-side reading of insider and outsider positions is moot and Western authors and readers are unlikely to change their views of Africa and Africans. Above all, African children who have access to these books would continue to see themselves through this predominant lens as they grow into adults.

However, hooks situates this complicity within the theory that Westerners' modes of seeing, thinking, and being are hegemonic—that is, that they serve society unequally. The representations of West Africa in children's books seem to make Africans' efforts to modernize invisible to all who are not there. Part of this modernization process began with movements to resist colonial rule over most of Africa during the first half of the twentieth century. This independence is something the West does not appear ready to accept.

Rather, they choose to believe that West Africa remains a set of unnamed colonies. In children's books, this version of reality is what publishers and authors expect their readers to accept. Of course, this view of Africa makes it easier for Westerners to accept when the "first world" continues to intervene in African affairs and transnational corporations export Africa's natural resources and enjoy cheap labor.

The people of Africa are worth knowing. They are not anthropological artifacts to be preserved in literary museums. They are groups of people and cultures, who are as dynamic as those of the rest of the world. Their development has not been arrested. I do not dispute the warmth and hospitality that the village setting implies, but the village should not be the only setting for African stories, and it should not be romanticized by and for colonial masters who miss the "good ol' days." The simpler life of Africa that children's books most often project were also subjugated lives, lived by Africans whom the world considered to be less than humans.

The people of Africa deserve better than this. We must stop erasing Africa's colonial past within traditional tales and we must stop ignoring Africa's current development. We must stop hegemonic seeing and thinking about Africa.

Part II
Growing Up African and Female in Children's Books

Black Woman, you have always been there, leading the way
　　Without you I would not stand here, as I stand today
　　I don't know how you do it, how you keep on going
When away from you so many of my brothers are roaming

　　You've been raped, ravaged, had your name defaced
　　Yet still you've found time to be the backbone of our race
　　The backbone of our race, our heart, and our foundation
　　Even when we were stolen and forced to build a nation

. . .

　　I thought I was alone, with no one to accept me
I turned to you and you were mad, but you didn't reject me
　　You never gave up on me, your love was so absolute
　　　　Even when I was angry and took it all out on you

　　I realize that I hated myself and that I did not hate you
　　　I just did not know how to appreciate you
　　　　　　(*From the Limbs of My Poetree* by Omekongo Dibinga)

Chapter Four
Religion and Childhood in Two African Communities: Ogot's "The Rain Came" and Adichie's *Purple Hibiscus*

Hard as some in the West may think, in many African communities children are highly valued and are considered the wealth of the family. This is because most Africans believe that as long as there are children their communities would never disappear. Thus their customs and traditions would continue to flourish long after their own demise (Mbiti, 1989). It is for this reason that many people within the culture tend to pity rich childless folks. What would such people leave behind when they are gone, is a question some ponder. This situation of materially well-off people with no children sometimes drives relatives to intervene in people's relationships and lives in strange ways. For example, some relatives may insist that their brother take in "a more fertile woman," or that their sister should sneak in a child in the relationship and pass him/her off as the man's. If the couple in question refuses to act accordingly and eventually dies, they become part of the village folklore and songs. In such songs the story of their fruitless lives is narrated as a cautionary tale to the youths who may underestimate the significance of procreation. Through this medium of oral tradition the youth are reminded, as John S. Mbiti (1989), a professor of African religion points out, that "children are the buds of [African] society" (p. 107). And also that for a woman not to be perceived as "the dead end of human life," she must produce an offspring (p. 107). There is no question then of how important children are in the African consciousness.

Paradoxically, children can also be sacrificed whenever it is necessary to protect the health of the community or the family, or to elevate the status of the father figure. Sometimes, this takes the form of what is popularly known as ritual killing, as parents and village elders attempt to ward off an evil spell that might be "affecting" the family or the village's fortune. Children then have to be sacrificed, partly because of their purity and innocence. Those selected for this "honor" are expected to understand that they are giving their lives up for a worthy cause; and that the adults in their community mean well. Perhaps sacrificing the child as a peace offering to the gods is the only way the community can stop the famine that would not go away; or maybe it is the only way to eradicate the disease that was ravishing the community. Thus it is better for the family and the village to relinquish a dearly loved child in order to sustain the community. This is because the effectiveness of the ritual would depend on the value of that child. Simply put," the community which . . . protect[s] the child, feed[s] it, bring[s] it up, educate[s] it," also reserves the right to sacrifice him or her to the gods (p. 107). Mbiti adds that such sacrifices are necessary to maintain an "ontological balance between God and man, the spirit and man, the departed and the living," for if this balance is "upset, people experience misfortunes and sufferings" within African traditional communities (p. 59). The only way these people know how to resolve such problems, as learned from past practices, is to sacrifice one of their own.

Ritual killing associated with traditional African religion is not the only way that a child's physical life and emotional health can be endangered in African societies. Religious extremism poses similar threats to children's lives. For example, there are situations where children have also suffered unnecessarily because of their rejection of Christianity. They are then persecuted by a father figure who may demand that they should not interrogate the teachings of the new religion he has embraced. If the children disobey, they may be physically abused or severely punished. Although such persecutions may appear to many as less offensive than ritual killing, they also have the potential to destroy children. For not only can continuous persecution affect the child emotionally, it can eventually lead to his/her death. In order to stay alive, the child then must succumb to the whim of whoever is in charge regardless of whether she/he subscribes to the teachings of that person's religious persuasion or not.

Childhood experience for some African children, like children from other cultures, can be as fulfilling as it can be challenging. This is what I intend to demonstrate in this chapter. What complicates African children's experiences, though, is the fact that they must contend with two or three distinct religions. Like their parents, they also wrestle with traditional and Christian or Islamic religions—religions imported from regions whose cultures they must learn to understand as well.[1] Furthermore, most of them do not really have a choice as to which religion they should practice, for as Mbiti (1989) points out, they are socialized to accept mainly the religion they are exposed to in their community.

Children of Christian converts in particular must therefore abide by the Christian doctrine or suffer the consequences for not abiding. And as usual, overzealous parents who may want badly to impress the church leaders or to demonstrate to the outside world that they are no longer "pagans" enforce these rules. This struggle can further oppress a child and cause him/her to rebel and eventually become self-destructive. Thus while the Christian converts in African societies may reject traditional religion for being "barbaric" and forbid their children from practicing it, the Christian alternative may inadvertently become "barbaric" depending on the African convert. When these converts follow the new religion blindly without separating its teachings from the Western customs inherited from missionaries, they not only confuse their children but can also hurt or kill them. This is one way Christianity can become "barbaric."

In the short story "The Rain Came" and the realistic novel *Purple Hibiscus*, the Ugandan and Nigerian authors, Grace Ogot and Chimamanda Ngozi Adichie respectively wrestle with these issues. They both capture the impact of religious extremism in the lives of two girls—one in a pre-colonial Ugandan village, Luo, and the other in a postcolonial Nigerian city, Enugu. Each author explores succinctly an aspect of childhood experience as it pertains to religious practices in some African societies: ritual killing and Christian fanaticism. The two images of African childhood they depict, although disturbing, are also two forms of religious persecution African writers like Chinua Achebe and Ngugi wa Thiong'o have dramatized in their highly acclaimed literary masterpieces, *Things Fall Apart* and *The River Between*. In Achebe and Ngugi's fictional versions, as in real life, the children actually die. Ogot and Adichie, however, provide alternative solutions to death for their female protagonists facing a similar predicament.

In the discussion that follows, I will demonstrate that decisions made by father figures in "The Rain Came" and *Purple Hibiscus* are motivated more by their dogmatic religious beliefs and an unconscious insatiable greed for power than by love for their children. Therefore, they are able to make decisions that serve mostly the needs of the larger community of which they are a part rather than the needs of their children. We notice this in the actions of Chief Labong'o and Eugene Achike, the father figures in Ogot's short story and Adichie's postcolonial novel.

Traditional African Religion and African Childhood

In "The Rain Came," Ogot tells the story of Oganda, a girl who is selected as an offering for the ancestors, so that the rains would come and enable the crops to grow. An emotionally charged story that reads more like a folktale, "The Rain Came" depicts how Luo, a pre-colonial Ugandan village, functions. When the story begins we meet Oganda's father, Chief Labong'o returning to the village after consulting with the rainmaker about their predicament. He is not happy, for "It is no longer a question of being the chief of hunger-stricken people that weighed Labong'o's heart. It was the life of his only daughter that was at stake" (p. 92). This poses a big dilemma for Labong'o. As a father it is his responsibility to protect his daughter; however, as the chief of Luo, it is also his duty to cater to the needs of his people. Not only is Oganda his favorite child, she is the only girl amongst his twenty children. Better yet, she is the child of his favorite wife.

Never in his life had he been faced with such an impossible decision. Refusing to yield to the rainmaker's request would mean sacrificing the whole tribe, putting the interests of the individual above those of the society. More than that. It would mean disobeying the ancestors and most probably wiping the Luo people from the surface of the earth. On the other hand, to let Oganda die as a ransom for the people would permanently cripple Labong'o spiritually. (p. 93)

Therefore, Labong'o has to choose what he believes is the better option. He chooses the village over the daughter he loves so dearly, privileging communal interest over family interest. This means then that even though losing his daughter would destroy him "spiritually" as he laments, he will have more credibility as the chief, for he has demonstrated that "his people" mean more to him than members of his immediate family.

Although one can easily deduce from the story that Ogot's sympathies lie with the girl who is about to be offered as ransom to the gods, she maintains a distance and lets Oganda speak for herself. This sacrificial lamb is then empowered to question the decision made by her father and the elders of the village. Thus, while relatives and friends "congratulate" Oganda, believing that it is "a great honour to be selected by the spirits to die, in order that society may live" (p. 95), Oganda, on the other hand, is outraged and gradually she begins to feel a deep sense of betrayal. The more she reflects about her predicament, the more she realizes that she had never really "understood" her people. "If they loved her as they had always professed why were they not making any attempt to save her?" (p. 96)

As the African girl she is within this pre-colonial village setting, she accepts her fate, rationalizing that, if it is what the ancestors have prescribed for her, then, so be it. However, as a child who depends on her family and her community for guidance and protection, she is still unable to make sense of the custom. She voices this concern as she sings on her way to the great evil forest where she is expected to offer herself to the lake master.

> The ancestors have said Oganda must die
> The daughter of the chief must be sacrificed . . .
> My age-group has consented
> My parents have consented
> So have my friends and relatives.
> Let Oganda die to give us rain. (p. 97)

Ogot does not provide an easy solution to this age-old custom. She stays faithful to the traditional practice but raises some doubts about such blind adherence to tradition. She also draws our attention to the different responses of the females in this community, exposing the pain of the bereaved mother, the hypocrisy of the co-wife, and the empathy of the little girl who is brave enough to offer Oganda solace on her journey to the land of the ancestors. Each one of these females is affected differently. The mother weeps and mourns, the co-wife celebrates, but the little girl who gives Oganda a present to give to her late sister already in the ancestral world empathizes.

The magnitude of what may be considered as family and communal betrayal makes Oganda numb to the point that when Osinda, a young man who loves her, eventually disguises himself as a creature of the forest, tries to rescue her, she pleads with him to let her die. She seems not to care anymore, for as she explains to him she has to die or else, "the eyes of the ancestors will follow [them] everywhere" (p. 99). As they both escape from the great forest the rain begins to pour, which according to the custom means that Oganda is finally with the ancestors. Although the sacrifice Ogot describes here turns out to be symbolic, Oganda still loses her innocence and must begin her life burdened by this "near death" experience.

Perhaps ending the story in this manner is Ogot's way of revealing how absurd the custom is. Or maybe it is her way of seeking a compromise, insinuating that children who are selected to become sacrificial lambs, with help can always find a way out. As demonstrated in the story by Osinda's actions, they can accomplish this without humiliating their elders or without ridiculing their tradition, for as Mbiti (1989) acknowledges, "religion is the strongest element in traditional background, and exerts probably the greatest influence upon the thinking and the living of the people concerned" (p. 1). It does not matter whether this same religion requires that its believers kill someone on its behalf.

Ritual killing or human sacrifice is a sensitive subject among African scholars who are also skeptical about the Western cultural practices that have overtaken our people. Africanist scholars continue to analyze this practice in literature as they try to understand its significance. Ngugi wa Thiong'o (1997) comments generally on the contradictions of some of these traditions but is also unable to offer easy solutions. He notes that "certain normative values in a so called national or communal culture could be reflecting all sorts of contradictions of which it is a product" (p. 126). Ogot, in a way, questions this blatant contradiction of sacrificing a child one loves, especially since children are "buds of society" (Mbiti, 1989, p. 107).

In *Things Fall Apart*, Achebe explores a similar contradiction in a compelling manner, showing the complexity of traditional African religion. In this classic novel, Ikemefuna (Okonkwo's protégé) is eventually killed because the Oracle of the Hills and Caves says he should be sacrificed. Therefore, even though Okonkwo is extremely fond of this boy, he is unable to stop the process. Rather, he participates when he is not even expected to do so, consolidating his power base within the village community (Booker, 1998). Emmanuel Obiechina (1975) links the actions of villagers to their spirituality and survival and notes that the spiritual leader is indeed very important in the village. He remarks further that:

The earth for an agricultural people is the primary source of sustenance and so holds the key to survival. Therefore, its priest is easily the most important religious (and because religion permeates every facet of social life, social) parsonage in the community. If the earth goddess is angry and refuses to reward the agricultural effort of the people, crops fail and there's general misery. The man who propitiates her and acts generally as intermediary between her and the people is naturally a most powerful personage whose pronouncements in his official capacity cannot be easily set aside. With this in mind, it is easier to accept what may appear to the modern reader the traditional callousness and brutal cynicism of some of the actions in *Things Fall Apart.* (pp. 212–213)

If we apply this statement to "The Rain Came," which is set in East Africa, we can also conclude that the most important person in Luo is actually the rainmaker. He is more important than Labong'o the chief because he is the intermediary between the people and the gods. All the chief does is simply execute the orders from the spirit world. This is how Labong'o rationalizes not stopping his daughter from being sent on a journey to her expected death. However, in going along with the rainmaker's decision like Okonkwo, he is consolidating his position as the ultimate patriarch in Luo, a man to be respected and admired for his integrity and staunch belief in traditional religion. He is, therefore, the model leader and father for the community to emulate.

The only characters in Ogot's "The Rain Came" who are openly baffled by this tradition of sending a young child to the evil forest are Oganda and Osinda. Oganda, the protagonist, is very vocal about it and tries desperately to reason with the villagers, in vain. Ogot uses her to express a deep concern about the culture of sacrificing human beings for the well-being of the larger community. Rather than let the child wander off in to the forest alone, she develops an equally heroic character in Osinda to put an end to what seems like an absurdity to these youths. This way, Ogot is able to end the story on a hopeful note with the young couple abandoning their village for an unknown destination; it is also then that the rain actually comes. Thus where Oganda's father fails as the protector of his loving daughter, Osinda succeeds as the protector of his loving bride to be.

This custom of sacrificing humans, or the attempt, continues to exist in some modern African societies. Recently, the practice of ritual killings has gained the attention of the BBC as the law enforcement officers in England have begun suspecting some Africans of trafficking young children to Europe solely for this purpose (BBC News, 2003). In a 2004 documentary, *Multi Murders: The Dark Side of Occult Belief,* the ritual killing of a Benin boy residing in London is linked to close relatives. According to a South African spiritual healer interviewed for this documentary, the fact that the London authorities found the boy in red shorts symbolizes that the relative is apologizing for sacrificing him and hopes that when he returns to earth he will forgive this relative. BBC News also reports other ritual killings within continental Africa (2003, 2005). It has, therefore, become a common practice no longer associated only with the old world and the villages. People who celebrate ancestral worship should be very careful as to how they go about it, for as in most religious practices this form of worship can be abused by overzealous followers who want to exploit it for their private gains. When this happens, instead of strengthening communities, these same spiritual leaders may be destroying them. The religious practices of communities should not be taken lightly, for they can foster a certain degree of conformity that may undermine reason and logic.

Christianity and African Childhood

Africanist scholar Obiechina (1975) rightly observes that contemporary readers may find some of the practices associated with traditional African religion shocking or "brutal." This attitude comes perhaps from the fact that in modern society many Africans no longer condone traditional African religions. Instead, as Adichie (Vawter, 2004) remarks in an interview, they perceive the Christian religion as "far more superior." What some of these African believers do not realize is that Christianity, if taken to an extreme, can also be a problem. This is because as several Africans embrace the new religion brought to the continent by European missionaries, they tend to reject ancestral worship and anyone associated with that practice.[2] Traditional African religion is then dismissed carelessly as primitive and barbaric. The Christian converts, as Obiechina (1975) notes, "were obsessed with their own importance and contemptuous of all non-initiates" (p. 219). As stated earlier, Christian religion interpreted by overzealous fanatics can equally be "barbaric." Adichie demonstrates this in her award-winning novel *Purple Hibiscus*. Unlike "The Rain Came," the story takes place in postcolonial Enugu and moves back and forth between Abba and Nsukka. The key conflict here is between Christians and traditionalists, as represented by Kambili Achike's wealthy father and her humble paternal grandfather Papa Nnukwu.

The story is about a fifteen-year-old girl, Kambili, who suffers persecution at the hands of her father for loving her grandfather who does not practice Christianity. The novel opens with the following: "Things started to fall apart at home when my brother, Jaja did not go to communion and Papa flung his heavy missal across the room and broke the figurines on the etagère" (p. 3). This clearly echoes Achebe's classic novel and in a sense acts as a continuation to the Igbo struggle to live with "two" conflicting religions. The tension builds up when the family go to Abba to celebrate Christmas with their village relatives. This is where Kambili begins to understand how deeply her father feels about traditional African religion. Eugene Achike is a hard worker, a God-fearing man who believes strongly in social justice, yet he has little patience with people who do not practice Christianity. From his perspective, his children should have nothing to do with such people, including his father who holds on guardedly to the old religion. As he later explains to them, "My father spent time worshipping gods of wood and stone. I would be nothing today but for the priests and sisters at the mission" (p. 147). He is forever grateful for this and wants his children to remember and expects them to strive for perfection to please the Christian God.

Told from Kambili's point of view, the story revolves around major Catholic rituals and holy days. Each day Kambili's father aspires to do what he believes to be right in God's eyes. He is a devout Christian, a humanitarian, and a well-respected entrepreneur in the community. At home, however, his obsession with the Christian teachings drives him to abuse his family, especially his daughter whom he loves dearly. He does not hesitate to beat her, starve her or forbid her from interacting with her grandfather. Ironically, he does this simply because he does not want the child to imitate or imbibe "pagan" ways. It can be argued that it is this love for his child and his Christian God that makes him want to be perfect, makes him want to raise perfect children, and that also makes him want to do what he believes is the right thing for Kambili. Thus, what kind of a father would he be, if he does not guide her to the "right" religious path? All these said, he does not, however, see the error of his ways or that he is systematically destroying his loving family. During an interview with Norah Vawter (2004), Adichie remarks that she imagined Eugene "as a complicated man, a compli-cated father" who hits the daughter "because he needs to show her the right way." To accomplish this goal, he does "horrible things in God's name and [his] actions seem right to [him]."

Kambili longs to be in touch with her grandfather and seeks to understand his religion that has been rejected by her overzealous father. Because of what the grandfather symbolizes to the postcolonial Igbo community, Kambili is persecuted by her loving father, and is physically abused until she almost dies from broken ribs and other wounds. Fortunately for Kambili, she has her aunt, a professor who is able to give her some perspective on the two forms of religion: traditional Igbo religion and Christianity.

Adichie's protagonist, like Ogot's, idealizes her father and seeks to please him constantly. She wants to be the perfect student and daughter for him. When they drink their usual tea as a family, her dad's favorite beverage, she feels "the love burn [her] tongue" (p. 31). Eugene Achike is not only a devout Christian, but is an ardent purveyor of Western civilization inculcated in him through his Western education and religion. He is an example of what Christianity has to offer to African "pagans," the ultimate ideal African everyone admires or respects: family man, wealthy man, civilized man, and a humanitarian.

Like Oganda, Kambili gets help from people other than her father. In particular, Father Amadi nurtures her spiritual health in a different way. Adichie develops the character of this young African priest to show a different approach toward Catholicism in Nigeria. Unlike Father Benedict and Brother Eugene Achike, Father Amadi is down-to-earth and willing to listen to the youths, answering their questions about religion and life. He is not a special parishioner as are the other two, and does not mind that there are people in Nsukka who practice traditional religion. He is simply there to serve his Christian community as best as he can, hoping that people would convert without being coerced. Where her father fails, Father Amadi succeeds by showing Kambili a different kind of love that nurtures the whole person, as he encourages her to seek out truths for herself before making a decision as to what path to take.

Fathers, Religion, and African Childhood

In *Purple Hibiscus* Adichie equates traditional African religion with Christianity, something she says has infuriated several African readers, who believe whole-heartedly in the superiority of the Christian religion. Ogot, however, tries to maintain an emotional distance in her depiction of traditional religion and its impact on the life of her characters. Both authors succeed, though, in demonstrating the complexity of the religious experience. From these works we are able to see how religion can make well-intentioned fathers inadvertently hurt their families as they struggle to privilege the interest of the larger community of which they are a part. Ogot and Adichie also show how the young female characters respond to their plight. Oganda accepts her fate grudgingly, while Kambili starts off being passive because she is blinded by her love for her father. As the novel progresses she rebels against what she considers to be an obsession with the Christian religion manifested by her father, and almost loses her life. Why should she not keep the painting of her late grandfather in her room? Emboldened by the thought of preserving Papa Nnukwu's memory against all odds, she defies her father openly for the first time.

> I took the painting out of the bag and unwrapped it. Jaja stared at it, running his deformed finger over the paint, the finger that had very little feeling . . . I knew Papa would come in to say good night, to kiss my forehead . . . I knew Jaja would not have enough time to slip the painting back in the bag, and that Papa would take one look at it and his eyes would narrow . . . And that was what happened . . . What is that? Have you all converted to Heathen ways? (pp. 209–210)

Of course, Eugene Achike takes the bait and destroys the painting. When Kambili still refuses to let go of the remnants of the painting, he kicks and slaps her non-stop until she sustains a broken rib and bleeds internally. It is after this escapade that Kambili's mother finally intervenes by poisoning his tea, the ultimate colonial symbol.

> The phone started to ring. It rang for a long time; the caller must have dialed a few times before Mama finally answered it. She came into the living room a short while later . . . "They did an autopsy," she said. "They have found the poison in your father's body." She sounded as though the poison in Papa's body was something we all had known about, something we had put in there to be found, the way it was done in the books I read

where white people hid Easter eggs for their children to find . . . When she spoke, her voice was just calm and slow. "I started putting the poison in his tea before I came to Nsukka. Sisi got if for me; her uncle is a powerful witch doctor" . . . My mind was blank, I was blank. Then I thought of taking sips of Papa's tea, love sips, the scalding liquid that burned his love onto my tongue. "Why did you put it in his tea?" I asked Mama, rising. My voice was loud. I was almost screaming. "Why in his tea?" but Mama did not answer. (pp. 290–291)

The tea that Eugene Achike relishes and drinks religiously finally kills him. Even his Christian religion could not save him from the magic of the witch doctor's potion. The tea, like his Christian religion, slowly destroys the perfect family he has worked so hard to keep in check and eventually his obsession with the Western beverage becomes his own undoing. From this, readers can infer that Adichie privileges traditional African religion over Christianity, even though she uses Father Amadi's character to counterbalance the overzealous converts like Kambili's father who persecute their children. Thus traditional African religion may seem strange at first, but as Kambili realizes later after observing her grandfather meditate at her aunt's house, it is quite simple. Christian religion, which has been a major part of her life on the other hand, seems not only complex but also confusing at times to the fifteen-year-old girl. Adichie insinuates in the novel that Christianity is so because of its Western origin. Hence, it is difficult even for highly educated and materially successful African characters like Eugene Achike to fully understand how to implement the teachings right there in Enugu. And if such characters lack a complete grip on how the teachings should be applied in an African context, then how can they guide their children successfully without hampering their emotional or physical health? In a sense, she questions Achike's credibility as the ideal Christian convert because he fails to realize that his Western education and eternal gratitude to the missionaries who had made this education possible have blindsided him. So if he cannot see clearly, how can he act wisely? This is a theme that runs through both works of fiction.

Both fathers in "The Rain Came" and *Purple Hibiscus* can put an end to the sufferings their daughters undergo. They love their children and like Okonkwo in *Things Fall Apart*, they are fiercely protective of these children. Somehow, they are unable to free themselves from the hold of their respective religions. Chief Labong'o cannot stop the rainmaker sending his only daughter out into the evil forest to die for the community. But then Osinda, a younger man who is in love with Oganda is able to do so. Perhaps this is possible because he is not yet blinded by tradition and the power that goes with enforcing its rules. Eugene Achike cannot nurture or understand Kambili's love for her grandfather Papa Nnukwu, a man he considers a "heathen." On the contrary, he physically abuses her repeatedly, choking her with his obsessive and controlling love, and eventually almost kills her.

Why are these two fathers blinded by their religion? Is it because they love their village or Christian community more than their children? Or is it simply an unconscious obsession with power? For example, what would have happened if the chief had simply told the rainmaker that he would not allow the elders to send Oganda into the evil forest to confront her death; or that perhaps they should seek other solutions to the drought and famine problem that persist in the village instead of attempting to sacrifice an innocent child? Likewise, what would have happened if Eugene Achike had simply told members of his Catholic community that his father is a traditionalist, or just let his children enjoy the warmth and love their grandfather generously offers to them? These are difficult questions to ponder, for spirituality, although a communal affair in African villages, is indeed still a private affair for most people.

Another troubling question has to do with the position the mothers take. If we assume that the fathers' actions are motivated by a greater sense of responsibility that goes beyond the family, what then really motivates the mothers' inaction in these literary works? Oganda's mother is merely weeping and wondering why the Oracle chose her only child. Even at this crucial moment her sense of justice is still flawed. She cannot "rejoice" like the other women, yet like her husband she is unable to intervene (p. 95). Perhaps it is because she actually believes that appeasing the gods is right for the community, but it would be better if only it were another woman's child! Kambili's mother, who has also suffered as much as her daughter, however, is able to act. Although readers may not condone her approach, they can at least respect her for trying to save her children. At the end of the novel her family is far from perfect as Eugene Achike would have preferred, but the children can see their options more clearly now. They can practice traditional African religion or practice Christianity. However, they do not have to use only the colonial model of Christianity like their father. The mistake that Eugene Achike, whom I may refer to here as a "colonialist," makes, is in believing that he knows his children too well. As Achebe (1995) points out, colonialists such as him may feel that "understanding [their children] and controlling [them] went hand in hand" (p. 58). They do not seem to realize that wielding power over anyone, regardless of their race, ethnicity, gender, nationality, or age can backfire. The dominated person can only take that much before he/she snaps as she/he seeks ways to liberate the "self."

African children may have to decide for themselves just how rational their families' and communities' methods of protection or guidance are. They would have to understand what is motivating certain actions by the ones who love them. They may not fully understand certain traditions, but it is necessary that they seek full knowledge before rejecting an African paradigm for the Western alternative. This is because if followed blindly, each has the potential of becoming deadly, as Ogot and Adichie have demonstrated in their literary works. Whether African scholars like the images of African childhood presented in these works of fiction or not, they would have to agree that these female authors have done some justice to it. Granted, there are other images of African childhood out there that still need to be captured in literature. It is my hope that more African authors would depict other images of African childhood, so that we are able to understand how African children navigate their way through life's winding paths to adulthood.

Chapter Five
Revising Traditional Cultural Practices in Two Picturebook Versions of African Folktales

After discussing two different childhood experiences in the previous chapter, I feel it is necessary for me to also also show how children work with adults to bring change, so their culture would continue to thrive. This is because as many anthropologists would agree, culture, indeed, is the backbone of every community. From Ngugi's (1997) perspective, it is "a product of a people's history, [and] . . . also a reflection of that history." Culture has sustained us Africans from generation to generation and strengthened our sense of self and our understanding of our place within the global community.

There is no question then about its relevance in our lives. However, as I pointed out in Part 1, culture also perpetuates ways of seeing, behaving, understanding and knowing among groups of people. As these practices prevail over a long period of time, they become traditions that may be hard to challenge, practices that people cling to without question. This phenomenon seems to be true in several West African villages. For example, in recent years we hear that young girls from some parts of Africa are being punished severely either for acts of passion or for outright refusal to undergo circumcision rites of passage, which were the custom in the past. This has led to all kinds of conflicts, global and local, which could perhaps have been prevented if the elders had re-examined rituals of female circumcision inherited long ago from our ancestors.

What complicates matters further is the fact that well-intentioned Afrocentric movements in the West uphold all African village practices as "authentic," which seems to mean that they should not be interrogated or adjusted to suit contemporary reality. Afrocentric scholars argue that these village practices, in a way, are the only significant aspects of African culture not tarnished by Western colonial influence (Asante, 1985). According to these scholars, village cultural practices retain the true flavor of African tradition and have been faithfully adhered to for centuries. Although, as Oyebade (2003) remarks, Afrocentricity searches "for those values that will make man to relate to man in a humanistic way and not in an imperialistic or exploitative way," its persistent adherence to pre-colonial ways of doing things can be problematic. Should African children accept every single tradition that has been handed down to them by their elders? It is true that some traditional practices have sustained Africans for generations, but it seems to me that others are so inflexible and outright unjust that it would be irresponsible not to interrogate them. It would be better if elders assisted children to identify and re-examine cultural practices that are no longer useful within their different communities, as they guide them on how to create new traditions that do not violate our African "cultural integrity" or disrupt our staunch belief in ancestors. In so doing, children could learn to pay attention to differences that position us as "others" within our local communities and make us targets for practices that simply reflect the dominant ways of understanding, knowing, and valuing our humanity.

In recent years some authors of children's books have attempted to accomplish this feat in their folktales. At the centre of the folktales by Obinkaram Echewa and Nelda LaTeef, for example, is a child protagonist sharing space within rural settings with adults, negotiating relationships with them, and actually reasoning with them to rethink certain dominant cultural practices.

The Ancestor Tree

In *The Ancestor Tree* (1994) Obinkaram Echewa brilliantly depicts the struggle between old and new ways in Amapu, a West African village community. In the story an old man, Nna-nna, who regularly tells stories to the village children and showers them with his "blessings," cannot have an ancestor tree planted in his honor when he dies, because tradition forbids childless people from having trees planted in their names in the Forest of the Ancestors, and he has no living biological children. Worse yet, his navel tree "will be cut down from the Forest of the Living." In essence childless people should not be remembered, regardless of their contributions to the community.

This is a tradition that baffles the young children he has spent his entire life taking care of, and they are forced to question the usefulness of that tradition. Wasn't Nna-nna their surrogate grandfather? Has he not been there for them any time of the day? Refusing to accept this aspect of their village custom, they consult with the elders and eventually plant a tree in his name.

Echewa weaves this tale as honestly as possible, as he makes blind adherence to tradition appear foolish even to the elders, who at times lose their temper when asked about details of the customs:

> Inside their homes, when they were with their fathers and mothers or uncles and aunts, the children kept asking, "How come Nna-nna can't have a tree in the Forest of the Ancestors?"

"It is an ancient custom," Abindu's father said when Abindu asked him.
"How come there is such a custom?" Abindu asked.
"That's just the way things are. Custom is custom is custom," Abindu's
father replied.
"Do customs ever change?" Abindu asked.
"Enough questions!" Abindu's father replied angrily. (unpaged)

It is the village tradition, is the only answer the children are offered. Traditions
are fine, but when it makes people outsiders in their own villages, one begins to
wonder. Sindima (1990) remarks that, "in African thought, community includes
the living, the dead, and the unborn." Quoting Dickson, he continues:

> ancestors are important in African culture because "they . . . give a sense
> of solidarity and security . . . mediate between God and man [and] remind
> the living of those virtues which define the morally good life."

Would it not make sense then to honor Nna-nna, the village storyteller and
caregiver? Should he go unrecognized in village history, despite his endless
contributions, simply because he is childless? The intergenerational link between
the old man and the young people becomes an effective tool to address an
injustice that had been perpetuated by this tradition for a long time.

Echewa's story demonstrates the need for change. As the reader follows the
evolution of the story, he/she observes the stupidity of adhering to customs
that perhaps never made sense, even though they continue to be upheld in the
community. When the children succeed in effecting change in this community
after meeting with the Amapu village council and convincing them, the reader
is filled with a sense of joy. The eldest member of the council, Ozurumba,
proud of their dedication to Nna-nna and their commitment to social justice
remarks:

> Teach and learn. Usually, adults teach and children learn, but in this
> case, we have the opposite. Children are teaching and adults are learning.
> You children have taught us that customs have a beginning, customs can
> change, and sometimes, customs come to an end. We have decided to
> end one custom and begin another. We will plant a tree for Nna-nna in
> the Forest of the Ancestors. It is true that he has no children, but it is also
> obvious that he has left something of himself in all of you, which, after all,
> is what it means to be an ancestor. (unpaged)

The children have finally made a difference in a community that has practiced
for ages and without question customs that exclude honorable members of
their own village. Their action liberates the elders as well, for as Ozurumba
acknowledges:

We have also decided that, from this day onward, we will change the way we select which ancestors to honor. Beginning today, only people who have lived honorable lives, people whose spirits are noble, will have trees planted for them in the Forest of the Ancestors. Ezi, amuru indeed! (unpaged)

The Hunter and the Ebony Tree

Nelda LaTeef's *The Hunter and the Ebony Tree* (2002), though not as compelling as Echewa's tale, depicts a similar situation. In this story, a concerned father must "choose the right husband for his daughter." According to the village custom, it is the father who must initiate this process, but LaTeef adds a twist to the tale. After deciding that it was time for his daughter to be betrothed, the father "shared his concerns with her" and actually consulted with her on how they should proceed. What makes the story even more fascinating is that he listens to her suggestions carefully and does not quickly dismiss her as only a girl.

The girl participates in the courtship process, something unheard of in the past. She provides useful advice to her father on how to proceed, making it easier for him to perform his task as an elder. To her father, she confides that she "will marry the man whose arrow can penetrate the trunk of the ebony tree." She both understands her father's sense that it is his duty to find an appropriate husband for her as tradition dictates and appreciates his willingness to include her in the process. As a true African child, she does not disrespect him. He is not only her father, but also an elder and deserves nothing less. Rather, they work as a team. Even then she knows she must defer to him whenever necessary.

Many Africans may doubt the credibility of the father-daughter partnership depicted in this folktale, especially since it is portrayed by an outsider, but it is clear that Nelda LaTeef wants to make a point about involving females in the process of choosing their spouses. And so, instead of naively challenging the arranged marriage custom that is prevalent in traditional African societies, she provides an alternative way that acknowledges the girl and at the same time does not threaten or disrupt the community. LaTeef gives the girl agency throughout the story, even though she is a child and female. She makes it possible for her to accidentally meet with the man she eventually marries, to show the role that fate plays in such circumstances:

As the hunter stopped by the village well to quench his thirst, there, drawing water, was the girl. With a shy smile, she offered him a drink from her jug. She had never done that for a stranger before. The hunter gazed into her eyes as he drank the cold water. When he finished drinking, he knew his search for a bride had come to an end. (unpaged)

In a sense, rather than marrying a man who just won a contest, she ends up with someone she had earlier shown kindness to and perhaps is attracted to—a "husband who was worthy of her" and had used all his ingenuity to win her hand in marriage.

This folktale, which LaTeef got from an old Zarma griot, like Echewa's, rethinks tradition. Again a child becomes instrumental in a major decision process, this time in the village of Tombakonda. Some Africans may be skeptical about children tampering with our tradition. This is because most of us seem to pay attention mainly to the strengths of the culture and never closely examine its weaknesses. And of course, a communal lifestyle in the village is much to be preferred to the individualistic quest for materialism that is pervasive in cities and towns highly influenced by colonialism and Western culture. This notwithstanding, undue reverence for tradition can impede communal and individual growth, which in turn can be detrimental to otherwise thriving African village communities.

Conclusion

If we do not examine past practices and make decisions regarding which traditions to maintain and which ones no longer serve our human ideals, we could find ourselves excluding and oppressing a sizable segment in our communities. As Ngugi (1997) rightly observes,

> Certain normative values in a so-called national or communal culture could be reflecting all sorts of contradictions of which it is a product. In many African societies for instance, there are proverbs that essentially belittle women. And yet proverbs are supposed to contain the kernel of collective wisdom. (p. 126)

It is true that proverbs communicate cultural understandings about a group of people, but I am not sure African women would want to hang around permanently for their husbands and sons to "belittle" them in the name of tradition. I would suggest that Africans do what Aegerter (2000) advises in her article on womanism—and that is to "revise and retain African traditions" for the benefit of all segments of the community (p. 67).

How do we effectively challenge the injustices of colonialism when we are unable to address similar concerns about our local cultural practices? Such rigidity stifles progress, oppresses people, and encourages massive exodus from otherwise thriving communities. Finally, it reduces the individual to nothing, as he/she abandons all that is familiar and begins to wander all over the world seeking another place to call home.

As Echewa remarks in an interview (Kauffman, 1995), we do not need to "sanctify all traditions simply because they were passed down" to us. We need to uphold those that serve our communities well and reaffirm the members' beliefs in our humanity. To stay strong, healthy, productive, and alive, we need to constantly monitor our actions within our respective communities and examine our customs for loopholes. If we do not engage actively in revising practices that are detrimental to our collective survival, our children will not only draw these to our attention, but may be forced to change the traditions however they choose to. This can be dangerous!

Chapter Six

African Girls' Sexuality in Selected Fiction for Young Adults

In her 1997 article, "Controversial Issues in the Lives of Contemporary Young Adults," Shelley Stoehr remarks that "Many young adults have sex. They always have and probably always will. We can only hope they are safe and responsible" (p. 2). This may seem obvious to several people; however, most young adult books that explore this theme usually end up on the banned books list. This is because sex remains an uncomfortable subject among many people (Martin, 1999; Paul, 2005; Sheffer, 1997). As John Clarke (2004) points out, "sex and sexuality are topics that excite embarrassment and controversy" (p. 89). Therefore while in reality many may find pleasure in the act, there is a certain amount of guilt that is equally associated with the practice. Clarke (2004) further identifies four different aspects pertaining to sex and sexuality that capture this ambivalence. He notes:

> [S]ex is a *biological fact about human bodies*. We have specialized organs and body parts (genitals, breasts etc.) directly linked to the process of reproduction. There are other secondary sexual characteristics, such as body shape and body hair, which biologists argue arise out of our reproductive role and play a role in sexual attraction. Secondly, sex describes a *range of activities* (sexual intercourse, oral sex, masturbation) which use these sexual characteristics, sometimes to bring about reproduction, sometimes solely for pleasure. Thirdly, sex is a range of *social and personal meanings* given by people to what they are doing. Is this activity right or wrong? Is it sinful or holy? Is it consensual or forced? How does it make me feel? Does it give me pleasure? This leads on to a fourth element of sexuality—that of *sexual orientation*. Are the objects of sexual desire the same sex as me or different? (p. 89)

From this quotation it is easy to see why most adults are confused as to how to discuss sex with children. It is a delicate topic that must be approached with care lest we send the wrong message to our children, especially adolescent females. Furthermore, as Sheffer (1997) notes, "When we do talk to adolescent girls about sex . . . we discuss danger and disease, pregnancy and rape and what to do to protect oneself from these things" (p. 1). She argues that we should help girls to balance sexual "desire and safety"; this way we are not simply pretending that sex is all about danger or getting into trouble. It is also about pleasure, or what some may refer to as experiencing the "good feeling."[1]

This is exactly what some authors of young adult literature set in the West have attempted to do. To engage teens in the dialogue on sex and sexuality, they have depicted a wide variety of experiences ranging from sex as a pleasurable experience, as can be seen in Judy Blume's *Forever*, and Aidan Chamber's *The Toll Bridge* and *Postcard from No Man's Land*, to sex as a violent experience, as can be found in Chris Crutcher's *Chinese Handcuffs*, Sandra Scoppetone's *Happy Endings are All Alike*, and Saphire's *Push*.

As some Western authors seek constructive ways to address adolescent sexuality in fiction, most African authors either steer away from the subject completely or if they deal with it at all become didactic about the negative aspects of the experience. One reason for this is perhaps because, as Osa (1995) notes, romantic love in general is not considered an important subject in African children's literature. Thus if romantic love is not perceived as important to most African authors of children's and young adult literature for various cultural reasons, sex as a subject then would have to be off limits as well. This is because, as Osa explains further, "traditional African culture does not encourage high school teenagers to have girlfriends or boyfriends, and it frowns on dating among them" (p. xxvi). The implication is that although African teenagers are expected to eventually get married, the dating ritual is unnecessary, for it may lead to issues of sexuality not usually talked about in our culture. This may inadvertently account for the paucity of books that actually deal with African teenage sexuality. This notwithstanding, there are a few African authors who have dared to explore the themes of romantic love and sexuality in their books for young adults.

In her recent article, "Developing Fiction for Today's Nigerian Youth," Virginia Dike (2005) identifies specific Nigerian authors who have explored these themes as she remarks on the effectiveness of their representations and the impact such representations could have on adolescent consciousness. She cautions, however, that even though a few Nigerian authors attempt to write about love and sex, "there is very little that is romantic about most of these novels" (p. 11). This she attributes mainly to the fact that the authors simply "describe dismal relationships characterized by infidelity, exploitation, and self-centeredness. While others are cautionary tales of women gone astray" (p. 11). She also concedes that there is the need for more literature that features adolescent protagonists and experiences that mirror present-day Nigerian society—literature that depicts realistic peer relationships.[2] This problem is not limited only to Nigeria. Authors of children's books from other African countries including Cameroon, my country of origin, tend not to give much thought to themes of romantic love and sex as well. And if at all, it is almost impossible to find copies of such books published locally abroad, the context for the books I will discuss in this chapter.

Three Nigerian authors who have explored the theme of African girls' sexuality in their young adult novels (the primary focus of this chapter), and whose works are readily available in the West are Sefi Atta, Cyprian Ekwensi, and Buchi Emecheta. They have done so in their respective novels, *Everything Good Will Come* (2005), *Motherless Baby* (1980/2001), and *The Rape of Shavi* (1985). There are some Western authors who have also embarked on this journey to capture images of what they consider to be African girls' sexuality in their young adult novels. Some of them have won major awards for this endeavor. Without interviewing each one of these authors I can only speculate on their reasons for developing an interest in African adolescent girls' sexuality. For some, perhaps the controversy surrounding certain cultural practices linked to sex within Africa may have captivated their interest. Others may simply be curious as to how HIV is affecting these youths' sexuality, especially since Dike notes that African authors are not exploring this social issue in their books for adolescents. Regardless of the reasons, there are more Westerners writing about African adolescents' sexuality than Africans. It becomes necessary to see what they emphasize in their novels and how their characters—adolescent and preadolescent—respond to different aspects of their sexuality or their developing sexuality.

I have identified eight novels: three by Nigerian authors, and five by Western authors (Americans and Canadians). The stories are set in Kenya, Malawi, Nigeria, Sierra Leone, a generic African country, and a generic southern African city. The publication dates for these novels range from 1980 (original date) to 2005. I selected these novels purposefully from a list of 50 books I had earlier read for my dissertation and from the list of books submitted for review for Children's Africana Books Award (CABA) awards in the United States.[3] Given the sensitive nature of sex and sexuality, I wanted to understand how authors who write about African teenage experience depict African girls' sexuality.

After reading through the eight books I could find that explore this subject exensively I have concluded that literature that depicts African girls' sexuality dwells on the negative. What I mean by this is that adolescent readers do not get a balanced sense of the sexual experience. Rather, there is a deliberate attempt to frighten them about the danger posed by their sexuality, just as Sheffer (1997) has observed, or at times, there is some degree of cynicism communicated about sexual relationships, as Dike (2005) has pointed out in her study of youth literature published in Nigeria. In essence these authors suggest that when African girls engage in sexual activity or are being prepared for it, they suffer from some form of trauma or distress, be it emotional, physical, or cultural. Sex then has nothing to do with romantic love or with pleasure. Rather, it is an activity that jeopardizes one's emotional, physical, and cultural well-being. According to these authors, it cannot be a pleasurable experience because many African girls are subjected to female genital mutilation, which in turn can cause life-long emotional distress; or because sexual intercourse can lead to an unplanned pregnancy, which will also wreak havoc to the girl's emotions throughout her life. It will also expose these African girls to sexually transmitted diseases such as HIV and gonorrhea that may eventually cause their early demise or render them barren. Worse yet, because of their threatening sexuality, some of the authors insinuate that African girls are easy targets for rapists who may be living right in their own backyards. In their desperate attempts to communicate their different messages about African girls' sexuality, most of these authors become didactic. This has grossly affected the overall quality of some of their books as the stories seem contrived, or sound more like a series of campaign lectures about the pitfalls of engaging in sexual activities within African communities.

Sex as a Source of Emotional Distress

By far the most popular image depicted of African girls' sexuality is that of sex as a source of emotional distress. There are two ways sexuality can cause emotional distress as identified by some authors: through female circumcision and through unplanned pregnancy. In the first case the authors seem to point out in their stories that these females will not be able to derive pleasure from sexual intercourse when they become women because of the prevalent African practice of female genital mutilation they are forced to undergo. In the second case the author reminds girls that premarital sex will clearly lead to an unwanted pregnancy that may mess up their entire lives.

While one of the authors focusing on female genital mutilation finds the custom appalling and barbaric and makes sure the characters condemn it, others approach it with caution masking their true sentiments about the practice. Regardless, each author succeeds in reducing African girls' sexuality to a basic issue of clitoridectomy. The three novels that capture this image are Cristina Kessler's *No Condition is Permanent* and *Our Secret, Siri Aang,* and Rita Williams-Garcia's *No Laughter Here.*

In the two novels by Kessler the issue of female genital mutilation is quite evident. However, while she makes it the primary focus of her story in *No Condition is Permanent* (2000), it is subtle in *Our Secret, Siri Aang* (2004). In the first novel she tells the story of a fourteen-year-old white American girl, Jodie's reaction on finding out that Khadi, her Sierre Leonean friend, would be circumcised during a ceremony organized by the Sande Society. Jodie is appalled by this practice and is determined to prevent it from happening to her friend. However, she and her mother are forced to flee Bukama village and the country when her interference puts their lives in jeopardy. Although it is essentially a story of intercultural friendship, Kessler uses the relationship to comment on what her teenage character considers to be the absurdities of the Sierre Leonean customs. In essence she shows how two girls of the same age deal with their bodies and sexuality. While the one from the West has complete control over her body, the one from Africa seems resigned to her fate as she willingly agrees that her genitals should be mutilated for the benefit of her future husband. The saving grace in this novel, however, lies in the fact that Kessler, through the American mother figure character, expresses her disapproval of Western interference to obstruct traditional African cultural practices. However, readers, like Africana scholars Yusila Amadu Maddy and Donnarae MacCann (2002) can still notice that "the Western women (Jodie and her mother) are represented the way Western feminists typically represent themselves: educated, modern, as having control over their own bodies and sexualities, and the 'freedom' to make their own decisions" (p. 95, as quoted from Mohanty).

Thus Western authors like Kessler seem to harbor the belief that they and their adolescent girls have a greater control over their sexualities than do African girls. Readers get this clearly when Jodie's mom explains the process to her, equally expressing the disgust that as an anthropologist she has carefully masked throughout her stay in the village. She explains about the process: "Besides a helluva lot of pain and high rates of terrible infection? It can also mean sterility, as well as making sure that the woman never has any pleasure during sex" (p. 105). Sex then to Khadi would have no purpose since she may never find pleasure in the act. In addition, if she actually becomes sterile, motherhood is out of the question as well. This is a powerful pronouncement that can frighten any Sierre Leonean female, or make her peers from other cultures pity females from their country and from others that condone female circumcision.

Kessler's next novel *Our Secret, Siri Aang* (2004), set in Kenya, explores an African girl's sexuality in a different way. Like *No Condition is Permanent* (2000), the story stems from her journal entries as a Peace Corps volunteer in Africa long ago. Therefore, even though she is telling a coming-of-age story of a Maasai girl, Namelok, her Western consciousness taints the experience constantly. When the story begins and unfolds, readers meet a very independent twelve-year-old girl who is not only intelligent but quite adventurous and assertive. She wanders off to the wilderness on her own and does not hesitate to openly challenge certain aspects of the Maasai culture. Right away the reader gets the sense that this character epitomizes an African version of a Western feminist or environmental activist, even though she does not know it yet. Namelok hates poachers and makes it her duty to protect an orphaned baby rhino. It is against this backdrop that Kessler sneakily introduces the circumcision issue. Readers later learn that Namelok wanders off most of the time because she wants to postpone her "*emuratare.*" She has her doubts about this traditional rite of passage to womanhood, for it would curtail her "other freedoms" and she does not hesitate to voice this sentiment publicly (p. 100). However, she can express her concern only after listening to a radio program—a symbol of Western

modernity—that encourages young women to challenge such outdated practices. She believes quietly that even though many of the womenfolk may despise
her for the outburst, "they will respect [her] one day soon when not a peep passes
from [her] foolish mouth during the *emuratare,* or during each birth of all the
children [she] will have" (p. 104). Clearly, in this novel Kessler has simply made
her African protagonist a spokesperson for the West. Although Kessler dwells
heavily on the issue of procreation that is linked to the circumcision process in
this novel, she insinuates the deprivation of pleasure when she mentions
Namelok losing her "other freedoms" (p. 100). Readers are left to believe that
an African girl's life is empty without sexual pleasure. Kessler captures this as
she emphasizes the exotic aspects of the Maasai culture throughout the novel.

William-Garcia approaches the subject of female genital mutilation
differently in her novel *No Laughter Here* (2004). Unlike Kessler, she does not
hide her disapproval of the practice. However, like Kessler, she starts off by
forming a relationship between two young girls from two different cultural
backgrounds: African and African-American. Victoria and Akilah's friendship
is put to the test when Victoria Ojike returns to New York after a visit to Nigeria,
her country of origin, where she had participated in a circumcision ritual. Life
between the two prepubescent girls is no longer the same. However, as Akilah
desperately seeks different ways to restore her best friend's cheer she uncovers
Victoria's secret. From this point the story focuses on how Akilah's mother could
remedy the damage already done by a custom that requires "All proper Nigerian
girls" to perform what Akilah's mother considers as a barbaric ritual, in order
to "stop the good feeling" girls are expected to get from sexual intercourse
(pp. 72 and 108). In her quest to save this "emotionally damaged girl," Williams-
Garcia's American mother figure almost loses sight of the issue at stake here,
for readers may get the impression that she is more concerned with the "good
feeling" circumcised girls may lose from the ritual than with the possible infec-
tions that may accompany the mutilation process. Although I understand the
character's outrage, I still find this aspect of the novel disturbing in the sense that
the author seems to be communicating that without the ability to gain pleasure
from sex, African girls risk unhappiness. Sex therefore becomes an experience
that causes emotional distress.

Another book for adolescents that depicts this image is Cyprian Ekwensi's
(1980/2001) *Motherless Baby.* Like Kessler and Williams-Garcia, Ekwensi
emphasizes the emotional distress African girls face in regard to their sexuality.
However, as the title of his book suggests, he focuses on a variation of such
distress as he demonstrates that sometimes, emotional issues linked to sex are
brought upon the girls by themselves when they engage in premarital intercourse
and become pregnant. Ekwensi's story for the most part simply serves as a
cautionary tale to all adolescent girls whose strong desire for sex with a male
they may be infatuated with can impair their judgment.

In this novella, seventeen-year-old Ngozi finds herself pregnant after sleeping
with a popular musician who has multiple girlfriends. Since she is afraid of what

her parents may think of her, a secondary school girl having a child out of wedlock, and of the stigma that comes with this experience, she decides to abandon him at a cemetery. Readers notice that Ekwensi does not consider abortion as an option here. Rather, he allows his protagonist to carry the child to term and only then worry seriously about the errors of her ways. Before dropping the child (Pedro) off for someone else to take care of, Ngozi

> studied the lovely skin of the baby boy . . . That accusing gaze made Ngozi feel very guilty about her plan to abandon her first child. But Ngozi like all people who plan evil, consoled herself by saying to herself, "I am not committing any crime. I am doing what is best for the child. If I leave this child someone with money picks him up and trains him. I have done no wrong." (pp. 2–3)

And so she abandons the child. What is sad about the experience is Ekwensi's take on the issue. While he absolves the musician from any wrong-doing, he consistently regards Ngozi as a "wayward" girl who deserves whatever punishment lies ahead for this act against an innocent baby. In a predictable manner, when Ngozi grows up and settles down as a respectable wife in her Nigerian community, she is unable to conceive any more children. Despite her numerous consultations with medicine-men and her active participation in church, she is denied the opportunity to become a mother again. As the story ends, Ekwensi's female protagonist has suffered tremendous emotional distress throughout life for the mistake she had made that brought forth a child that is considered a "motherless baby" throughout the book, even when he is adopted by loving parents. Ngozi can find peace only when she admits the wrong she had done to Pedro publicly as she lay dying, for she "was no longer the little girl of seventeen with no knowledge of the world. She had lived and suffered, and she was still suffering on her sick bed" (p. 79).

Even though the story is contrived, Ekwensi's message to adolescent female readers, that sex is a great source of emotional distress, remains clear. This theme of how to deal with an unplanned pregnancy according to Denise C. Banker (1995) is very important to adolescents. As she notes in her article on abortion and young adults in the United States, "it may be the most important decision they ever make. No matter what the outcome, it may well affect them for the rest of their lives" (p. 1). Ekwensi attempts to communicate this same message to his adolescent female audience as well, although he chooses to explore the alternative of child abandonment that may perhaps be considered a lesser evil than abortion within a Nigerian context. However, he does so in a very didactic manner that compromises the artistic component of the book.

Sex as a Source of Physical Distress

A second major way authors have represented African girls' sexuality in young adult literature is by linking it to death. Thus engaging in sex will expose these girls to sexually transmitted diseases such as HIV that will eventually kill them, if they do not take better care of themselves. Allan Stratton and Deborah Ellis portray this reality in their award-winning novels *Chanda's Secret* (2004) and *The Heaven Shop* (2004).

Allan Stratton's *Chanda's Secret* is a powerful story about one family's struggle to live a dignified life amidst poverty and disease. Told from a sixteen-year-old girl's perspective, the author dramatizes the trials and tribulations of growing up female in a postmodern fictional southern African city. The greatest strength of this story is Stratton's ability to humanize AIDS victims. They are people like everyone else (our parents, relatives, friends, neighbors, etc.) and we must not discard them simply because they are gravely ill. However, the sub-message to the adolescent readers who are his primary audience is that girls in this community are at risk and must learn how to take charge of their bodies. If they cannot do so due to circumstances beyond their control (for example, if a stepfather takes advantage of a child as Chanda's does), they should at least know where to seek help or else they will die! Without question, sex as depicted in this novel is a major source of physical distress. Chanda must take care of her mother who is dying from AIDS contracted from an unfaithful husband; she must also take care of her HIV-positive friend who contracted the virus from the streets; and finally, she must protect herself against further assault from unscrupulous men as she educates the community about the virus.

When the story begins we meet Chanda in a funeral home making arrangements for the burial of her little sister who has just died from complications from AIDS. Her stepfather " is dead drunk at the neighborhood shebeen" (p. 3), and her mother is extremely depressed. The fast-paced narrative spares no detail as the author exposes readers to how imperialism affects African men and women, and also how patriarchal values grounded in traditional African practices are reinforced by Western capitalism in cities where adolescent females become the prey. In as much as Stratton attempts to complicate the story by weaving this strand of cultural imperialism and its effects on the local residents within his story about sex and the adolescent female in a fictional southern African city, though he tends to moralize a lot at certain points, he succeeds in telling an engaging story.

Deborah Ellis's *The Heaven Shop* (2004) explores the same theme, only her story is set in Malawi and targets a slightly younger audience. This novel, which provides crucial information about the AIDS epidemic in Malawi, is also engaging as readers watch with trepidation the gradual disintegration of a once thriving middle-class family. This family's ordeal exposes us to the devastating effects that the HIV virus has on the fictional Malawian communities depicted here. Told from a thirteen-year-old girl's perspective, readers learn how orphaned girls contract HIV from the men they entertain as they struggle to make a living to support other family members. Binti Phiri's sister Junie, a teenage girl full of dreams at the beginning of the story, becomes a victim by the end, for as an AIDS worker conveys to Binti, Junie has been sharing "a small house with several other women" who entertain truck drivers and has now tested positive with the virus (p. 169). Although this revelation shocks Binti at first, she is quick to realize that her sister's new lifestyle had predisposed her to this condition. But she is still saddened not only by this new reality but also by the way AIDS has ravished their entire community. What kind of future would she have with such a deadly disease looming around, she worries constantly.

As in *Chanda's Secrets*, adolescent readers can notice that sexuality throughout this novel is associated with AIDS the killer disease, although they can also see different ways AIDS victims give meanings to their lives. Ellis ends her novel with Binti coming to terms with their current reality as she remarks that:

> Since then, Binti had cried for her father and for her grandmother. There were almost certainly more tears to come, because life and love seemed to require tears from her, just as they required hard work and hard times, and keeping on when she wanted to give up. (p. 178)

These two novels capture the reality of sexuality in contemporary African society, which can be stated simply as death awaits any person, especially any adolescent girl who dares to have sex. This is a powerful message that can make anyone pause and reflect before he/she engages in a sexual relationship. But then how should adolescents deal with their pending sexuality? This seems to be Dike's (2005) concern as well, for as she notes about Nigerian youth litera-ture,"[t]he self-centeredness, opportunism, infidelity portrayed in the novels [Nigerian] is not the whole story but the picture is all true to life" (p. 11). She would like to see alternative images of relationships depicted in adolescent novels about Nigerians—healthy relationships that communicate to adolescent readers that HIV is out there no doubt, but one can still have a meaningful sexual experience with a loved one that is not necessarily a death sentence. I share similar sentiments and do believe that literature with such images is necessary not only to Nigerian youth but to all African youth. However, until this happens sex remains a source of physical distress.

Sex as a Source of Cultural Distress

Adolescent African female sexuality is also depicted as a major source of cultural distress. By this I mean that repeated betrayal by sexual partners is bound to make adolescent girls cynical about life and their environment. It can also render a culture barren, for these girls may unknowingly transmit STDs to men and the cycle continues. Readers can infer this from Sefi Atta's *Everything Good Will Come* (2005) and Emecheta's *Rape of Shavi* (1985). Atta's novel, which targets a general audience rather than only an adolescent audience, chronicles the experiences of a young girl over a period of three decades. Divided into years starting with 1971 and ending in 1995 when the narrator is a grown woman, readers follow Enitan's journey from an inexperienced sexual being to one who understands and is in control of her sexuality. To reach this point Atta consistently parallels Enitan's relationship with her parents and her closest friend Sheri. Readers become familiar with the girl's struggles as she tries to understand the definitions of loyalty and fairness within her Nigerian settings and seeks ways to forgive herself and her dad, and to find her place as a sexual being within a culture that has stripped almost every female of her dignity. The females in this fictional Nigerian society are simply sexual puns to the men they love, hate, or feel indifferent about. Men like sex, so give it to them, Atta seems to communicate in her novel; beware however, that they will always betray your trust and love.

Enitan the protagonist learns this very early when she is fourteen and stumbles onto a scene when her close friend Sheri is being gang raped. Her friend is taken advantage of, her mother is consistently disrespected and betrayed by her father who has numerous extramarital affairs, and eventually Mike the young man she loves and willingly gives herself to betrays her trust as well. It becomes easy therefore to conclude that adolescent females will constantly be betrayed through sex. This nasty "truth" inadvertently causes them to lose faith in the adults within their community and in their culture in general that condones sexual abuse of females. In a sense, Enitan wonders if there is any redeeming aspect in a culture that allows its men to take advantage of its female folk. If so, how can men and women live in harmony?

In telling the story of this young girl's awakening to her sexuality, Atta explores romantic love, demonstrating that it is really possible for adolescents to have a healthy relationship if they truly want. However, Atta does not dwell on this for long, for that sense of betrayal overpowers this message of love that could exist. Atta writes, "Sheri already had a boyfriend in school. They had kissed before and it was like chewing gum, but she wasn't serious because he wasn't" (p. 55). The author also explores the initial excitement that comes from having a crush on a boy. All these come to pass too soon as readers are eventually exposed to the gang rape scene on page 63. After the rape, Enitan cannot help but blame Sheri.

> If she hadn't smoked hemp it would never have happened. If she hadn't stayed as long as she did at the party, it would certainly not have happened. Bad girls got raped. We all knew. Loose girls, forward girls, raw, advanced girls. Laughing with boys following them around thinking she was one of them. Now I could smell their semen on her, and it was making me sick. It was her fault. (p. 65)

Sheri becomes pregnant and almost kills herself. Although she loses the baby, she is never the same again. The trauma has robbed her of her glow, her trust, and her freedom to assert herself. She would rather be a rich man's mistress now, since there was no joy in loving or having sex. Give it to them willingly and they will take care of your material needs, so she explains to Enitan. In 336 pages adolescent girls learn that in Atta's Nigeria sex is equated with treachery, pain, and numbness. There is nothing magical about the experience. Although the novel reads more like a cultural tour guide, Atta's point about the role of sex in the life of a Nigerian girl is clear. She seems to be trying hard to explain Nigerian customs and men to her Western audience. Her narrative, however, reflects a heightened adult political consciousness that from my perspective has affected the overall flow of the story.

All in all the reader is left with the image of cultural distress in regard to sexuality and the African girl. Simply put, if a girl loves someone and subsequently agrees to sleep with him, he will of course eventually betray her love. At times these girls do not necessarily have to wait for the person they love to sleep with them; some of those same males they hang out with would rape them, exposing them to ridicule. Sex is therefore a source of cultural distress—culture gone awry or out of control!

Buchi Emecheta's (1985) *The Rape of Shavi* takes a different angle. Unlike Atta's *Everything Good Will Come*, the adolescent female is raped by a white man, insinuating not only the physical rape but also a cultural rape of Shavi by the West. Basically, the rape of Shavi in this novel, which has been described as a "political fable of relationship between tradition and modernity," has great consequences.[4] Set in a fictional African country, Emecheta shows her readers how cultural misunderstanding or blind adherence to alien cultural practices can ruin an entire nation. In this case, Ronje, one of the Europeans whose plane happened to have crashed in Shavi, rapes fifteen-year-old Ayoko, a girl who has been selected specifically for Asogba, the heir apparent of Shavi. The reason he gives for ravishing this future queen is simply that "'*Black* people had no moral standards'" (p. 93). To prepare readers for this blatantly racist statement, Emecheta carefully builds a scene that suggests miscommunication, for as Ronje approaches, Ayoko "ran for the piece of cloth she had spread to cool in the dew and tied it round her waist. Then she saw who it was and laughed. Ronje laughed too, taking the laughter as an invitation" (p. 93). Having convinced himself that she is trying to seduce him, he rapes her, only to find out that she is a virgin! "Ronje fell on her and, in less than ten minutes, took from the future Queen of Shavi what the whole of Shavi stood for" (p. 94). Although the women of Shavi later punish him for this violation of their daughter and future queen, the damage has been done, for Ayoko contracts syphilis and eventually passes this on to her betrothed, who passes it on to his other two wives. Shavi is therefore left without a future since Asogba, the new King, is unable to produce children. While all this is happening on the domestic level, Shavi is also raped at the political level with Asogba instrumental to this cultural invasion as he embarks on a commercial trade with the Europeans, exporting crystals and relying on the Europeans to supply Shavians with foodstuffs. Not encouraging his people to rely on themselves for food as before leads to famine, which eventually wipes out most of the community. By the end of the novel readers not only see how sexuality can destroy an individual and the future of a nation, but are also forced to make a connection between cultural imperialism and the annihilation of a culture. Sexual intercourse is therefore a source of cultural distress.

One can therefore conclude after reading all eight works of fiction that engaging in or preparing for sexual intercourse can lead to an emotional death or distress as the protagonists who undergo female genital mutilation and Ekwensi's Ngozi who abandons her baby; it can also lead to physical death or distress as Chanda's mother experiences and as Esther, Chanda's friend who has contracted HIV may eventually experience. Finally, it can lead to cultural death or distress as Atta's Enitan and Sheri demonstrate, and as the Shavians in Emecheta's novel eventually realize. Sex therefore is not an experience connected with love, but one always connected with some kind of trauma (even when African authors write as insiders). Perhaps because sex is a sensitive topic (especially in this day and age of deadly diseases) this is the image of African girls' sexuality that authors feel comfortable depicting, as they may believe that these girls need to be protected from sexual predators and/or cultural conformity that may make them more vulnerable to exploitation and life-altering sexually transmitted diseases.

These reasons notwithstanding, is this all we want to communicate to our African youth about sex and relationships? Do we really expect them to believe that sexual relationships are this limiting? In that case, how do we encourage them to develop healthy relationships with young men and women in order to build a thriving community, which they will eventually become part of as sexually active adults—a community that is free of mutual fear and suspicion of each other's motives? As Virginia Dike (2005) rightly observes about Nigerian youth literature, "[y]oung people need all the help they can get in developing both physically and emotionally healthy relationships with the opposite sex and building a good foundation for family life" (p. 15). I agree with her that as authors continue to caution girls in particular about the danger of their sexuality, these same authors or new ones should attempt to present an alternative view of relationships, so that the girls have a basis for comparison. I feel it would be socially irresponsible to do otherwise, because fear alone does not protect our children from disaster, for when they get tired of being afraid they may leap blindly into a sexual world that will indeed kill them, as some of the authors discussed in this chapter have already indicated.

Chapter Seven
Individual vs. Communal Healing: Three African Females' Attempts at Constructing Unique Identities

Within the past decade, scholars and critics have identified and discussed various images of African womanhood in literature. Most often these include images of motherhood, wifehood, and other subservient roles linked to class and ethnicity.[1] These images are prevalent in the works of both male and female African writers. The differences lie, however, in their interpretations. Often, male authors hail African womanhood as supreme; hence, African women must be put on a pedestal because of the sacrifices they make for the well-being of their families and society. However, the female authors, for the most part, interpret the roles in relation to patriarchal oppression. To them, denying oneself other identities in order to serve fathers, brothers, husbands, and sons limits the woman in several ways. Consequently, African female writers like Buchi Emecheta, Flora Nwapa, Ama Ata Aidoo, and Mariama Ba provide alternative images of how women in different settings actually deal with this reality.

As African women struggle against roles assigned to them by patriarchal structures, their daughters must either accept the limited options presented as their ultimate destiny, or look for alternative identities in a world that nurtures, confuses, and at times destroys them. Their fight to maintain a "self" they feel comfortable with must begin at an early age. Like many of their mothers, these teenaged girls may choose to accept the limitations of their gender, or, like their fathers, they may continue to deal with the reality of being Black and African in a world still governed by Western values. As a result, depicting adolescent girls in literary works continues to be a challenge even to African female writers. As a compromise between what is expected of adolescent girls in their African communities and an ideal they should aspire to, some female authors marry teenaged characters to older, wealthy men as second wives, or to men of equal or better circumstances for protection. Some use teenaged girls to punish the men in their communities, and other authors depict girls sent abroad without their consent to pursue Western education.[2] Still there are some authors who let their African female adolescent characters live in their society, examine their options, and make tough decisions as they search for identities suitable for their evolving needs. Two authors whose works exemplify this are Tsitsi Dangaremgba and Zaynab Alkali. Their novels, *Nervous Conditions* (1992) and *The Stillborn* (1989), explore adolescent girls' quests for new selves in their respective African communities. These authors painstakingly describe the compromises these girls make to accomplish personal goals; their dilemmas in male–female relationships; and, when necessary, their constant struggle with what Joy Bostic refers to as "multidimensional oppression" (142).[3] The ability to assert one's identity without being crushed by the weight of indigenous and hybrid cultures cannot be overstated, for cultural crossroads can be treacherous places even for the bravest of people.

Adolescent Girls and Cultural Conformity or Resistance

Dangaremgba's and Alkali's female adolescent characters deal with multifaceted problems that are overwhelming even to the adults in their worlds of southern Africa and West Africa. Tambudzai in *Nervous Conditions* is a poor, teenaged girl who must make difficult choices in the midst of patriarchal, colonial, racial, and class struggles. Within the Shona culture, she is expected to abide by the patriarchal rules that govern her village and other local communities. In the larger context of her country, Zimbabwe, she must also deal with racial and class issues that perpetually make her feel like an inferior other to the whites and the wealthy. Her struggles are compounded by remnants of colonialism that inadvertently make her a beggar in her own country. Simply put, life in such an environment can never be fair.

In the opening lines of the first chapter, the reader meets a thirteen-year-old girl whose perspective on life may be regarded as shocking. Using the first person narrative, Dangaremgba presents Tambudzai's confession:

> I was not sorry when my brother died. Nor am I apologizing for my callousness, as you may define it, my lack of feeling. For it is not that at all. I feel many things these days, much more than I was able to feel in the days when I was young and my brother died, and there are reasons for this more than the consequence of age. . . . For though the event of my brother's passing and the events of my story cannot be separated, my story is not after all about death, but my escape and Lucia's; about my mother's and Maiguri's entrapment; and about Nyasha's rebellion—Nyasha, far-minded and isolated, my uncle's daughter, whose rebellion may not in the end have been successful. (p. 1)

At this point readers are immediately drawn to the protagonist as we wonder why this African teenaged girl professes to be so "callous." When we learn that there are few opportunities for her in her local community because of her gender, things begin to make sense. She can never dream of attaining any form of education until her brother, Nhamo, the natural heir in the patriarchal system of power, dies. It is an unwritten rule understood by every member of her immediate and extended family as well as the villagers. Her rich and educated uncle can sponsor only one of his younger brother's children as a gesture to uplift the social status of that branch of their extended family. Thus, even though Tambudzai is intelligent, highly motivated, and willing to earn money for her own schooling, her father, "a staunch traditionalist," considers her education a total waste of time (Punter, 2000, p. 152).[4] She is a girl and ostensibly should aspire to marriage and motherhood instead, as they are commonly practiced among the Shona people.

Nyasha, Tambudzai's cousin, on the contrary, has no problem with obtaining an education. Because her parents are highly educated and affluent, they are able to provide her with all the material things that she needs. Despite this, there are separate rules and expectations for her and her brother. Like her impoverished village cousin, she must defer to the males and maintain a low profile in order not to draw attention to herself. However, because she is not well grounded in either the village culture, like Tambudzai, or the Western culture, like the British girls she has met abroad while her parents pursued their education, she is an easy target for an identity crisis.

Zaynab Alkali's novel, set in northern Nigeria, also chronicles the plight of adolescent girls as they navigate between rural communities, whose cultural practices they are more familiar with, and cities fraught with vestiges of colonialism.[5] Li, the protagonist, and her friends must survive in a society that places higher value on males. Although her situation is not as complex as the one described by Dangaremgba, Li must also struggle to assert her identities as a female child growing up poor in a standard village, as a teenaged bride languishing without her husband, and eventually as a successful schoolteacher running her father's compound which has been abandoned by her brother. She is a young woman who expects much out of life and makes every effort to improve her social class through education and earn respectability among her peers within the village. However, she is still compromised by her gender as she suffers indignities from men who mock her and those who expect to have their way with an affluent, supposedly lonely young woman. In relating Li's experiences, Alkali exposes the futility of girls hoping for better relationships with men by constantly placing Li's dreams of social and gender equality beside her reality as a frustrated teenager and a neglected bride. This depiction reinforces her point that young women should come to terms with the fact that gender equality can be a hard thing to accomplish within patriarchal communities, especially the ones described in *The Stillborn* that are besieged by racism, classism, and colonialism.

Left, then, with little choice, Dangaremgba's and Alkali's adolescent females must seek alternative ways to survive their oppressive realities. The first and most important obstacle to social respectability for Tambudzai and Li, village girls with memories of acute material deprivation, is the lack of education. To liberate herself from the clutches of poverty that make her father "grovel" (p. 200) to Babamukuri, "an educated African" (p. 87) and "a revered patriarch" (p. 197), and become a young woman with more social recognition than she believes her uneducated and impoverished mother would ever have, Tambudzai must first conform and ignore the injustices she faces on a daily basis. She must then fight her family, suffer more indignities from colonial institutions, and alienate herself from the Shona culture, relatives, and friends she had loved dearly.[6] This is partly because she is embarrassed by the abject poverty she sees in the village and the way it strips the villagers (her parents included) of their self-respect vis-à-vis colonial products and icons such as Babamukuri. In essence, she must accept at least partially a system that is destroying her people in order to accomplish her economic goal. Education then becomes her only salvation.

Her pragmatism falls squarely in line with what Claudia Tate often refers to as "political desire"—that is, having a political identity forged through education for social respectability.[7] In her analysis of some novels that depict African-American experiences within the post-reconstruction era, Tate (1992) draws attention to the characters' desire to succeed materially against all odds. She notes, "money provides a very practical racial service for those in the middle class. Having money reduces middle-class black people's exposure to the more flagrant forms of racial discrimination" (p. 111). Thus, even though blacks with money continue to experience racism, it is, as with Tambudzai's parents, not in the crudest form that those at the bottom rung of the social ladder experience it. Hence, it does not surprise the reader that this teenaged girl's private ambition is to rise above her impoverished state. Colonial education is the only way through which she can accomplish this, even if it means that she ignores blatant racism at a boarding school.

Alkali's Li also believes that she can work her way out of poverty through the colonial means of education. She has planned to be a successful schoolteacher. As she reflects on this while doing the dishes in her father's house, "[t]he image of a big European house full of houseboys and maids rose before her" (p. 55). She eventually accomplishes this dream, but her reality as an African female familiar only with the northern Nigeria village ways of doing things continues to oppress her in different ways. When she marries at fifteen and eventually joins her husband in a city with her other "cast offs from the village," she feels like those people Patrick Hogan (2000) describes as "disrupt[ed]" by colonial contact (9).[8] Although highly educated by the village standards, she is insignificant in the new urban setting, where she suffers indignities at the hands of strangers and close family members who consider her provincial.

While Tambudzai and Li are willing to negotiate their identities initially on a material basis, Nyasha in *Nervous Conditions* expects and searches for an ideal self that should liberate her from the "multidimensional oppression" that African females face in this novel (Bostic, 1998, p. 142). She will not settle for any half-measures and does not want to be "entrapped" like Maiguri, her highly educated mother who insists on catering to her father's every whim. Her mother's chronic desire to please Babamukuri reminds Nyasha of images of female disempowerment explored by Western feminists in some of the books she has read. Consequently, she is infuriated and willingly discards her mother as a role model, without pausing to reflect on the real reason why a woman as highly educated and aware as her mother would continue to give in to blatant sexism in her matrimonial home. Andrea O'Reilly and Sharon Abbey remark in *Mothers and Daughters* (2000), an analysis of mother–daughter relationships within an international community that offers avenues for women's empowerment: "what the mother models for her daughters is therefore not necessarily success but struggle: an everyday lived resistance to the world that seeks to claim and control mothers and their daughters, a Demeter who rages, revenges, and reclaims the loss of her daughter to patriarchy" (p. 10). Maiguri therefore fails in this respect to render the emotional and psychological assistance her daughter needs in order to resist oppression by consistently letting Babamukuri impose Shona and colonial gender expectations on Nyasha. She must then live with the young woman's fury as a blatant symbol of her betrayal. Thus, Maiguri's inability to demand respect from her husband translates into weakness that Nyasha believes she may have inadvertently inherited. However, when Maiguri abandons her family for the first time in their lives, Nyasha is pleased and considers it a sign of hope. As she explains later to her cousin, who opposes her view on the issue, "there was a difference between people deserting their daughters and people saving themselves" (p. 173). By saving herself from patriarchal oppression, Maiguri is paving the way for her daughter's subsequent liberation. Nyasha's contentment is short-lived, though, for her mother seeks refuge, but from another male, her uncle.

Tambudzai is also disappointed in her parents, particularly Ma Shingayi. She considers her a failure because Ma is poor, uneducated, lazy, envious, and openly resentful of Babamukuri's patronage. Her mother's perpetual feeling of powerlessness leads to an interlude of depression that further alienates Tambudzai from her mother and reinforces her need for a new and separate identity. She "reproached [Ma Shingayi] . . . annoyed with her for always reminding [Tambudzai], in the way that she was so thoroughly beaten and without self-respect, that escape was a burning necessity" (p. 123). Running away from the village of her childhood, her mother's lethargy, and her father's dependency is the only way Tambudzai believes she can liberate herself from the disrespect and indignities she finds pervasive in this rural setting dominated by patriarchal values and colonialism. However, she fails to see the danger in her own pursuits as she salivates over colonial desires that negate Shona culture and continue to strip her immediate and extended family of their dignity as human beings, Shonaians, Zimbabweans, and Africans. It is a phenomenon

Ma Shingaya explains simply as the disease of "Englishness," brought to her home by her British-trained in-law in the name of upward social mobility.

Unlike Dangaremgba's girls, Li in *The Stillborn* sympathizes with her mother who has embraced the patriarchal institution wholeheartedly and expects her daughters to do the same. Her role had been reduced to one of taskmaster. Alkali writes,

> They heard Mama's unmistakable footsteps and stopped talking. . . .
> "Awa!" she called from the doorway. "Go fetch some water. Li wash the dishes. . . ." By now they had dispersed to their various chores, leaving her standing alone in the doorway. It was a routine instruction and never varied. Always the same words in the same order. . . . Even Mama's step as she walked away was mechanical. (p. 7)

Although Li always does her chores as is expected of young women within this culture, she also finds time to complain about the rigid rules that permeate the entire village community and reduce it, more or less, to a "prison" (p. 3). Her greatest strength is what her family refers to as the "stubborn streak" she has brought along with her from her mother's womb (p. 7). She uses this to challenge her father openly, and she points out instances of social injustice in their community. A reputation for being stubborn and at times clairvoyant helps her negotiate identity within the limited space allocated to her by her father who still wields power over them as children.

Post-colonialism and Cultural and Gender Identity

Chinua Achebe (1992) remarks in "Named for Victoria, Queen of England," that "[Africans] live at the crossroads of cultures . . . [and] have a certain dangerous potency; dangerous because a man might perish there wrestling with multiple-headed spirits, but also he might be lucky and return to his people with the boon of prophetic vision" (pp. 190–191). He argues that because of this reality, Western scholars expect educated Africans to be "torn" between these two cultures. Consequently, educated Africans would be judged incapable of providing guidance to their emerging youth population. Refuting this notion, Achebe professes not remembering "any undue distress" from the experience (p. 191). Rather, he was able to place Western culture into perspective as he retained his identity as an Igbo man at the crossroads.

Yes, Achebe was grounded in the traditional African way of doing things, which provided a buffer as he moved back and forth between the Igbo community and the Christian world that exposed him to Western civilization. He was also a male who already knew his place in the village social hierarchy (even as a boy); he definitely had more status than his female counterparts. Because of this strong sense of self as an African patriarch who is destined for greater things in his evolving community, he survived the cultural crossroads.

However, in one of his recent books, he insinuates that many Nigerians are still struggling.[9]

The adolescent girls in Dangaremgba's *Nervous Conditions* and Alkali's *The Stillborn* are not that privileged. Even though they also manifest what Simon During (1992) refers to as "the post-colonial desire . . . for an identity," by virtue of being female in their local African communities, this is almost impossible for them (p. 125). Their "cross-roads of cultures," as with other teenaged girls in our global society, have expanded beyond the two arms Achebe mentions in his article to include class and gender concerns as well.

In *Nervous Conditions*, Tambudzai's struggles for a new self begin in the village long before she comes into contact with the other "arm of the crossroads." Like Achebe, she is able to negotiate a self she values amidst the conflicting identities of peasantry, ethnicity, and wifehood, partly because of her village roots. Unlike Achebe, however, Tambudzai regards the village as a source of shame, deprivation, and indignity. It is a place where poverty reigns, women and girls come last, and rich relatives have no qualms about planning others' lives. Tambudzai, therefore, knows where the village is and understands the tradition but chooses a life of material privilege. Nyasha, on the other hand, does not have this option. She actually belongs nowhere. Growing up in England as a racial other, then living in post/neo-colonial Zimbabwe as a displaced young woman, and visiting relatives in the village where the local people despise them for bringing colonial chaos to their structured world but simultaneously admire their material success, Nyasha feels confused and overwhelmed at being a by-product of colonialism.[10] Consequently, she suffers the greatest "distress," for while "wrestling with multiple-headed spirits," she almost loses her mind and young life (p. 190).

Nyasha's struggles eventually alienate her from her parents and classmates, whose values conflict with hers and the Shona culture she understands very little of. She experiences her greatest loneliness and betrayal when her cousin leaves for boarding school and becomes part of the unjust system that breeds Africans like Maiguri and Babamukuri.[11] Nyasha can no longer hide from the obvious truth that she is different and perhaps displaced culturally from her environment and people. She loses the struggle with no one there to explain exactly what has gone wrong. Is it simply because she is intelligent or because she is an African at a crossroads? Perhaps it is because of being both of these, as well as being young, well-read, black, and female in a postmodern/postcolonial world that no longer offers clear solutions to cultural problems. She cannot pinpoint the single cause for her emotional, psychological, and physical isolation. Later in the novel she attempts an explanation to Tambudzai: "They think that I am a snob, that I think I am superior to them [classmates] because I do not feel that I am inferior to men. . . . And all because I beat the boys at maths!" (p. 196). In her isolation she lacks the ability to manage the decenteredness that comes with fighting unjust systems and simply laments, "[t]hey've taken us away. They've deprived you of you, him of him, ourselves of each other. We're groveling . . .

Daddy grovels to them. We grovel to him . . . I won't grovel" (p. 200). At this point she knows she is in trouble and would like to get help from a professional, but even this is denied her because of her race. "Africans did not suffer in the way [being] described," a white psychiatrist whom they consult tells them (p. 201).

Nyasha's illness, although interpreted as one of "Englishness" by Ma Shingayi, is evidence to Tambudzai that her decision to go to a racist school is a much more accommodating option than fighting structures and institutions that perpetuate injustice with no guidance. But in the end she realizes that her political desire for a respectable self should be balanced with human dignity. By rejecting the homestead and embracing the Western center that is destroying her people simply because of a political identity of social respectability, Tambudzai realizes she is no different from the African adults in her community she has spent endless nights criticizing.

For Li it is a different story. Even though she admires the city and its excessive materialism, she's quick to notice its destructive force. She can see what it has done to her once caring lover, whose decenteredness disrupts even her own life. Like Achebe, she has the village to run back to, where she eventually picks up the pieces and raises her daughter as a single mother. In this setting she regains her self-respect as a person, but continues to suffer from sexism as a female. Unlike Tambudzai, she embraces the contradictions that come with the territory. Thus, instead of shame, she enjoys her material success and ignores village customs that privilege men. However, as soon as the reader becomes comfortable with her choice, thinking that Li has finally overcome the gender oppression, she packs up everything and joins Habu again in the city. When Awa asks her why she's running back into the arms of a man who has consistently ignored and emotionally abused her, especially now that he's disabled, she replies: "We are all lame, daughter-of-my mother. But this is no time to crawl. It is time to learn to walk again . . . I will just hand him the crutches and side by side we learn to walk. . . . May the good God guide us all" (p. 105). This unexpected twist in the story confuses me as a reader. However, through further research I later learned that it was Alkali's way of imposing her *womanist* agenda on the novel. Gina Wisker (2000) echoes this sentiment when she postulates,

> Many of the tensions in writing by contemporary African women novelists are located in the relations between colonialism, post-colonialism and feminism. Post-colonialism and feminism are themselves seen to constrict and inform re-descriptions of the world, overlooking or not cohering with African women's lives and their negotiations between equality and self-development. (p. 132)

To Alkali, womanism is the appropriate lens through which African women writers can channel their messages.

Womanism and African Girls

Since the feminist movement began, many Black feminists have been ambivalent about its role in their lives.[12] In the search for a framework that would reflect their condition, "womanism" was coined. What exactly is womanism? According to bell hooks, "*womanist* connotes 'a black feminist or feminist of color'; a woman who, among other things, is audaciously 'committed to [the] survival and wholeness of entire people, male *and* female'" (quoted in Walker, 1983, p. 58).[13] As several womanist scholars would agree, the "healing" and "wholeness" of an individual and community are key elements of this philosophy.[14]

Certain events or occurrences in Dangaremgba's *Nervous Conditions* do not make sense through the feminist lens of an American perspective. For example, Nyasha is partly destroyed by the limitations of her own understanding of the force of "multidimensional oppression" (Bostic, 1998, p. 142). Her lack of a holistic understanding of the complexity of her fate as a young, educated, Black African female in a transitional postcolonial society shortchanges her greatly and makes her extremely vulnerable to the ailments she suffers in the novel.[15] Her insistence on hanging on to the binary ideologies of feminism and Black liberation that simply address gender and race as propagated in the West blinds her to her cultural reality.[16] As Bostic (1998) rightly observes, "White women may ignore the way in which they are privileged by their whiteness and black men are able to ignore the ways in which they are privileged by their maleness" (p. 144). Where then does that leave Nyasha, who must also deal with parental and colonial oppression, among other things? Her decenteredness baffles even her, for she actually believes she has the answers to the problems, having read several books on Western tradition and feminism. Consequently, she thinks she has a better chance of surviving cultural oppression than her cousin, who never traveled beyond the village until it was necessary.

Does the womanist perspective work for Tambudzai and Li? Perhaps so, because although we find them at the end of the novel still dealing with some form of oppression, at least they made the decision to be part of that particular system, which means they feel stronger. Tambudzai chooses to go to an obviously racist boarding school; Li returns to a husband who does not necessarily care for her, but she feels that it is a wonderful opportunity to start their marriage this time as equals as they "learn to walk" together (p. 105). She does this to maintain the family for her daughter, while Tambudzai makes the compromise in an attempt to empower herself materially so she can be free to deal with the other injustices. While I understand the reason these characters make the sacrifices, I do not condone any form of social injustice. But if one closely examines the situations among the three, it is easier to tell which of the three females would live on to carry the struggle forward. Definitely, it would be the two who have the village to fall back on. Perhaps this is what both authors are striving to achieve. As Lindsay Pentolfe Aegerter (2000) notes, Dangaremgba "wanted to reveal the importance of rural life to that of urban experience; she wanted to reveal the 'both/and' rather than colonization's 'either/or' of African experience" (p. 71). In the struggle to assert their individual identities, Tambudzai and Nyasha must then learn how to balance the old and new culture, making sure they reject injustices that threaten their very existence as "whole" human beings within a community that must be constantly checked.

Alkali once remarked during an interview that she deliberately tries to keep the African family and community together. As an African writer, she feels that it is her responsibility to do so if she is to be consistent with her womanist beliefs.[17] Although I see her point of view, I have my misgivings about the ending of her story. Li has much potential as a character, and yet she must give up almost everything she has worked for alone for the one man who consistently humiliates her. I do admire Alkali's Afrocentric ideals; however, as a human being, I am uncomfortable with a situation whereby a strong Black African female character is forced to sacrifice much of what she has accomplished for a male partner who betrays her repeatedly. Throughout the novel, Habu does not show or give Li the affection she deserves as a wife. Neither does he treat her with respect. However, he expects her to be there to pick up the pieces. Does this mean that African girls and women from the communities depicted in the two novels should accept emotional and psychological abuse from the men they love? What then is the man's role in this community where the woman must make endless sacrifices in order to preserve the family and community? Can she alone heal a community burdened with multiple forms of oppression? I do not think so, even if she is free from the troubles that plague the community, and this is unlikely. Does Alkali's ending mean that women and girls in rural northern Nigeria communities can be equal to men only when these males are down on their luck? Should these females wait until men have some kind of misfortune before they can actually demand the respect they very much deserve? These are just a few of the concerns I have about Alkali's novel, especially since she claims outright that her vision is shaped by her belief in womanism. Furthermore, going to the city that has destroyed Habu emotionally, psychologically, and physically, and leaving the village that is her cultural base could weaken Li as before. The difference this time, though, is the fact that she, her daughter, and Habu would live as a family for the first time. Perhaps Alkali is implying that as a family unit, together they will be able to withstand adversities much better than individually. This way Li is instilling a sense of hope in her daughter, the new generation.

There is no doubt that healing is very important to womanists. I do, however, hesitate to accept the notion that it is primarily the woman's responsibility to heal a community, even though Li has accepted the village ways of doing things, for as Aegerter (2000) rightly observes, "[w]omanism seeks to revise and retain African traditions" (p. 67).

This notwithstanding, it is absolutely necessary to emphasize the magnitude of the liberation task that lies ahead of us as we raise adolescent girls who are aware of the multifaceted oppression prevalent in our global community.[18]

These girls should be "courageous," "audacious," "willful," "serious," "responsible," and "in charge" (Bostic, quoted in Walker, 1983, p. 141). When Black African adolescent females are in charge of their own lives, then they will be able to survive the weight of the different forms of oppression confronting them on a regular basis. However, it is extremely important for them to also be able to identify specific social injustices and develop strategies suitable to combat them.

The struggle to establish identity still rages on as dominant cultural forces continue to dictate how girls should be socialized to behave in society and what they should expect from relationships with members of the opposite sex. They are also exposed to conflicting messages about race, class, and other issues that impact on their sense of "self." Despite this, we can still make a difference in small ways as parents and adults by modeling behaviors that are liberating and by refraining from further oppressing one another, and by asking readers to question these values in the books they read.

Part III
Reading African Cultural Survival in Children's Books

It makes sense to examine black American and black African writing together—not only for the mirroring which we can immediately notice, nor for the continuous bouncing back and forth between the two continents as in the case of Negritude writers, nor even because so much of the writing on these two continents shows such a clear parallel development. But, rather, we need to look at these works together simply because literature has never existed within a vacuum, because literature does not develop inside of closed national boundaries, inside of closed cultural areas. We can only learn from these two areas together.

(Larson, December, 1969)

Chapter Eight
Reading Images of Resistance in Tom Feelings' *The Middle Passage*

This project will not be complete if I do not include a chapter or two that emphasize our historical and cultural connections with Blacks in the diaspora. Although some critics may argue against this, I have come to realize that our fate as a people is, and will always be, linked. Thus asking the question what happened in the 1400s in continental Africa and what continues to happen today in the diaspora to Blacks becomes necessary. Interestingly when reading Donna E. Norton's *Multicultural Children's Literature* (2005) I also noticed that her timeline for African-American children's literature begins with the 1400s and stories about the slave trade (p. 14). Ngugi wa Thiongo (1997) also notes that "The most important collective experience for Africa and the world over the last four hundred years was the economic, political, and cultural dislocation of Africans under two connected historical phases: slavery and colonialism" (p. 139). The Black experience in the diaspora unavoidably needs to be part of this dialogue, especially as it relates directly to the African experience. We need to have some kind of tête-à-tête with each other to understand why White folks have historically, and repeatedly laid claim to our property, our "selves," and our children. And as Feelings (1995) has demonstrated, we need to get Black youths involved in this liberation project.

Of course, slavery is a difficult subject to talk about, especially with children and young adults. Writing about the transatlantic slave trade experience for young people can be challenging for obvious reasons. The subject is not only too sensitive and graphic in nature, but can evoke a sense of guilt/shame or deep anger even among children who have a limited understanding about slavery. Thus, most authors who attempt to depict this experience for children wrestle with what "TRUTHS" about the experience they should include, and how they should tell the stories. And as Africana scholar James Turner (2005) pointed out during his presentation at Bloomsburg University on the evolution of Black scholarship in academia, people are afraid to "challenge certain truths for fear of punishment." By people, he meant Black scholars. I would add that this statement could also apply to Black authors. Indeed, some Black authors of children's books who have dared to address "racial truths in their books" have suffered this fate. One way these authors get punished is through book sales. Unfortunately, this may not necessarily be the fault of the publishers. Rather, the general White public tends to shy away from certain truths about our collective human experience. When this happens, an author's book eventually goes out of print as in the case of Irene Smalls' *Ebony Sea* (1995). Her picture book about slavery depicts what may be considered as mass suicide by drowning of the Ibos as a form of protest. Because it disappeared within six months or so after publication many children's literature educators and scholars have never heard of it. Thankfully, Smalls has finally found a way to subvert the system by marketing and distributing a new edition herself. The subject of slavery must be addressed in children's books regardless of how the public feels about it. Not telling the story because of the painful nature of the experience is cowardly and can do us more harm. This is because "focused" dialogue can help facilitate the healing process as we make peace with our past, liberating ourselves to build a healthy future for our children.

One author who has taken the trouble to show just how complex he believes slavery to be is Tom Feelings. Like some Black scholars he also feels that it has greatly affected and continues to affect African-Americans today. His wordless picture book, *The Middle Passage* (1995) is quite elaborate in its narration of the events that occurred four hundred years ago. From his book readers are able to understand why there is continuous tension between Blacks and Whites. Although they may find it puzzling, they are also able to infer from the pictorial depiction why there exists some amount of tension between American Blacks and their African brothers and sisters as well.

The story Tom Feelings tells in his much acclaimed wordless picture book is not only comprehensive, but undermines what some Western White historians have documented about the transatlantic slave trade experience. Steven Feierman (1995) has already pointed out one blatant falsification about this experience. According to him, Fernand Braudel, a renowned historian had remarked that "European ships on the west coast met with 'neither resistance nor surveillance'" (1995, p. 44). What Braudel is implying therefore is that the African borders were always open to invasion, and that the people were incapable of protecting themselves from outside invaders. Therefore, anyone had the right to invade African villages, confiscate the villagers' property, and enslave the people. This perception has been challenged, of course.

Although several authors of picture books such as Kim Siegelson (1999), Ann Grifalconi (2002), Margot Raven (2004), Sandra Belton (2004) among others have written about or illustrated slavery, none has focused solely on the transatlantic slave experience. None has also succeeded in capturing the intensity of the emotional, psychological, and physical pain involved in the struggle as dramatically as Tom Feelings. Most often their slave stories dwell on one family's experience or one African ethnic group's experience. Feelings' wordless picture book goes beyond this. He explores the tragic fate of Africans who lived during a particular period of our human history, and how this experience might have shaped race relations in the United States. As Michelle H. Martin (2004) reminds us, "*The Middle Passage* works well to help ground students in the African American historical event in which African America began" (p. 186).

In *The Middle Passage*, Feelings demonstrates the complexity of the slave experience, challenging the notion that Africans were "passive and inert" as Fernand Braudel had claimed (cited by Steven Feierman, 1995, p. 44). To him, some Africans resisted in different ways, and these forms of resistance need to be documented. On first glance at the opening pages of his wordless picture book this resistance may not seem too evident; however, as one flips through the book it becomes blatant and gets even more graphic. That is how powerful his visual historical fiction is.

Why does he present such graphic images in a book format that typically targets very young children? Without interviewing him specifically on this issue, I can only make an informed guess as a Black scholar of children's literature, educator, and mother of Black children. Thus I believe that it is a strategy to get the attention of our youth who are already hooked on violent video games. I say youth because the subject matter and images are not developmentally appropriate for the very young that usually read wordless picture books. On the other hand, the shock appeal can force readers in middle school and upward to take a second look, or at least ponder the grotesque images of Black folks in shackles packed like cattle in the bowels of a cargo ship. Readers of all shades *will* be forced to respond somehow. Some may get really angry at the thought of seeing human beings so "denigrated," some may not even read through the visual images but would have to contemplate the little segment of the book they saw, and still further, others may start asking questions. Black children in particular can no longer hide from the fact that their current reality is linked to this historical event that we are all so ashamed to talk about.

Depicting the slave experience in such a blatant manner does not necessarily mean that Feelings wanted to "demean" Black folks. Rather, it is the contrary. Borrowing a quote Heather Sofield (1999) uses in her postcolonial analysis of Achebe's *Things Fall Apart*, I would say that Feelings' book attempts "to strengthen, not demean, [African-American] cultural heritage"; it is "a means to forge a new identity" (unpaged). The new identity created for Black youth involves resistance and tenacity as depicted in Feelings' book. The Africans he captures on his canvas resisted slavery, as some conspired with the slavers for social and economic reasons during the transatlantic slave trade. The conspiracy, according to John Henrik Clarke (1995), happened because "the Europeans devised a method of divide and conquer, pitting one African village against the others and then taking the spoils for themselves" (unpaged). John Thornton (1998) explains this conspiracy in another way. To him Africans were "unwilling participants" in the slave trade who did it for commercial purposes. Regardless of the reasons, there remains the fact that some Africans were part of the complicity.

Although Feelings addresses these complex relationships in his book, his primary focus seems to be on the sense of agency of the enslaved Africans throughout the journey across the Atlantic. He acknowledges the indomitable spirit of the Africans whose stories he is telling, perhaps to help young readers to better understand who Africans and African-Americans truly are—a race of people that can neither be destroyed nor eradicated completely from the surface of the earth. Thus racist folks can maim our bodies but they will never succeed in completely capturing our souls.

The notion of oppressed people having a sense of agency can be far-fetched to some, especially to former colonial and neocolonial masters who may want to hang on to the illusion that they have always been in control and will continue to hold their colonized subjects in check. This inadvertently may account for why "there are scrupulous accounts of western domination" and not enough documentation of oppressed people's "history of agency" among the colonized (Gyan Prakash, 1995, p. 5). This claim, though made about the colonial experience, can also be applied to the slave experience. This is exactly what I believe Feelings sets out to accomplish in *The Middle Passage*.

In this chapter I will identify and discuss three major ways Africans resisted their White captors throughout the voyage as depicted by Feelings in what Martin (2004) refers to as his "historically speculative wordless picture book" (p. 94). It would be naïve for anyone to actually believe that enslaved Africans accepted their fate without a struggle. After reading the visual images in Feelings' *The Middle Passage* carefully I identified three major forms of resistance:

1. Africans resisted through outright defiance.
2. Africans resisted through slave revolts.
3. Africans resisted through suicides.

Resistance Through Defiance

When the visual narrative actually begins, readers are exposed to a peaceful idyllic setting with Africans living their lives normally. This lifestyle is disrupted suddenly by what first appear to be Arab slavers, and eventually by what appear to be White slavers. But before the slave raids, we are exposed to the image of two African warriors (their heads) superimposed on a slave ship. Their heads seem larger than the ship itself. This image appears twice in the book. It is a powerful image that captures the rage of the African villagers who are not willing to go without a fight. It is such an effective image that in 2004 it was used to announce the "International Year to Commemorate the Struggle against Slavery and its Abolition" by UNESCO.

As the story unfolds, we are exposed to other manifestations of this defiance.

We notice that even though Africans are armed only with spears that do not stand a chance against the guns the slavers possess, they fight back relentlessly. This seems to echo the message in Claude McKay's poem, "If We Must Die." Some Africans in these preliminary pictures die fighting. Those taken by surprise do not just stand there to be captured. Rather, some attempt to run away and are shot in the back while others engage in physical battle with the slavers and/or their African middlemen.

Even in chains as the slavers and middlemen lead them toward the ship, Feelings' Africans refuse to succumb. Some are depicted holding their heads high amidst everything as others stare back at their captors in defiance. On the ship the rage seems to intensify as women also fight off slavers trying to rape them. Images of enslaved Africans screaming in their tight abodes in the bowel of the cargo ship are prevalent. The struggle continues throughout the crossing.

Resistance Through Slave Revolts

As it becomes more evident that the slavers would not let them go, the enslaved Africans must employ new strategies to overcome their fate. We notice this in a double-page spread illustration right after some Africans have begun jumping overboard. This distraction creates a fertile ground for mutiny. In this illustration, we see the slaves in chains rushing toward their captors. Some die in the process but so do some of their White captors. At the center of the double-page spread is a picture of an African choking his White captor, forcing his head to tilt backward. Fighting with their bare hands and in shackles, they do not stand a chance at winning, but this does not deter them from trying.

Slave revolts were inevitable. This resistance marker is common in several slave narratives. In fact, it is one of the most documented. Although their chances of succeeding may seem grim, the slave revolts demonstrate how far enslaved Africans were willing to go to seize back their freedom. Many authors have documented similar forms of resistance. For instance, Hugh Thomas (1997) lists the different rebellions that occurred during that period in his book, *The Story of the Atlantic Slave Trade: 1440–1870*. While identifying the 1532 slave uprising as one of the successful ones, he also remarks that "There was probably at least one insurrection every eight to ten journeys" (p. 424). Herbert Klein (1999) in *The Atlantic Slave Trade* adds that "slaves rebelled—sometimes successfully—on a total of 313 voyages and Africans on the coast cut off the slave ships or their boats on another seventy voyages" (p. 159). Howard Jones' *Mutiny on the Amistad* (1987) focuses exclusively on a particular slave rebellion.

One slave revolt I found intriguing at the Great Blacks in Wax Museum was the one led by Captain Tomba from Sierra Leone between 1693 and 1694. Watching these African wax figures (including a young fellow) strangling crew members was quite chilling and made me wonder what they might have gone through that would make them perform such violent acts on other human beings. But then again, standing in the bowel of a replica "cargo" ship in the museum that was packed with enslaved wax figures and merciless slavers gave the answer away. I needed no further explanation.

In the course of such revolts many unarmed Africans lost their lives; so did some of the White slavers who were permanently armed with guns, as readers can notice in the visual images in Feelings' *The Middle Passage*.

Resistance Through Suicide

Another form of resistance used during the transatlantic slave trade was suicide. Thomas (1997) discusses extensively the different ways Africans committed suicide in order to avoid becoming slaves in the New World. He identifies starving, jumping overboard, hitting one's head against the ship, and at times holding one's breath to "try and smolder" oneself as key strategies Africans used (p. 412).

The two primary forms of suicide that Feelings depicts in *The Middle Passage* are self-starvation and jumping overboard. Readers notice this right away. According to the images, when an African goes on hunger strike it takes at least three males to force-feed him. This particular illustration that runs across a page and a half, like all the illustrations in this book, is quite detailed. On the left side of the page is a picture of a slaver whipping an African to eat. Another leads a second African toward the center where three slavers are force-feeding a third African. It is not an easy process. A fourth African is lying on the ship floor and a couple in the background are either jumping overboard or attempting to do so. Indeed, the slavers are not finding it easy to feed or keep the Africans in check. Thomas (1997) confirms this when he remarks that "The hour of meals was the most dangerous time for the crews: four o'clock in the afternoon was 'the aptest time to mutiny'" (p. 420). The subsequent illustration is a double-page spread that forces the reader to watch Africans jumping overboard into shark-infested waters rather than become slaves. At the bottom of the ocean are skeletons of dead people—perhaps of former suicide victims. This demonstrates how determined they are to liberate themselves.

Feelings depicts the entire transatlantic slave experience as an ongoing struggle between the slavers who are heavily armed and the Africans stripped of everything, or taken unawares, or barely armed with weapons not as sophisticated. The portraits of the different male casts that Feelings parades on the border before the three last illustrations in the book insinuate not only hope but also equality. The African is positioned last and the slaver first. This positioning is significant for it suggests some kind of hope. The five White slavers and the five Africans look equally determined and ferocious. None seems willing to succumb.

Bishop (1996) also points out that, "even though shackles remain, [there] are signs of survival, signs of hope, signs of life" (p. 438). This remark pertains to the last pictures in the book—images of a family, "a woman holding a baby, the head of a child, a pregnant woman, a man sifting soil through his hand"

(p. 438). In addition, we see three Africans with what may seem like painted faces. There are long white streaks of paint running across the faces from the forehead to the chin. This may seem like "African warrior" marks, thus insinuating that although the slavers may have won that particular battle, the war is not over yet. As a matter of fact, it has just begun. Behind are fainter images of seven Africans in chains. Feelings, as Martin (2004) observes, "still emphasizes the strength of black people" as he conveys their "painful history" (p. 98) in these illustrations.

Understanding how our ancestors survived the numerous invasions of their homeland and how some survived the middle passage becomes relevant to every Black youth. It may further give us clues as to who we are, and help us sharpen our survival skills to suit our contemporary realities, be it in the continent or in the diaspora. As Blight (1999) notes, "We have narratives as an authoritative means of negotiating between retribution and forgiveness, between ignorance and knowledge, between lies and enlightenment" (p. 52). Feelings' wordless picture book is one such narrative. It enlightens us about an important phase of our historical past as Black people, identifying our treachery, our pain, and our strengths (physical and mental). Black children can learn to "appreciate their own beauty . . . and to recognize that the strength that enables them to survive is not an individual force but a collective one" (Sims, 1982, p. 98).

In summary, Black people will always be under siege; developing relevant skills to help us survive physically, emotionally, psychologically, spiritually, socially, and materially is of utmost importance. Thus, when scholars like Donna E. Norton (2005) simply see but the "pain of the slaves as they cross from Africa to the Americas," we should see more than this (p. 34). We should transcend these "portraits of loss and grievance" (Sofield, 1999) that others emphasize and instead capitalize on the portraits of "resilience" and hope provided by Feelings in his remarkable book, which not only forces us to look back in anger, but demands that we rise and reclaim our rightful place in the world as heroes. Remembering that our ancestors who were dragged across the middle passage died while fighting and continued to fight in captivity should empower us. Although their bodies were broken, their spirit remained intact. *The Middle Passage* is, therefore, a story of trauma from which we can learn tremendously about our racialized history. Like Black women's fiction, Feelings' book can also be compared to what hooks refers to as an "emotional trigger" (2005, p. xi). However, as hooks explains further about Black women, we should strive to go beyond the trauma in order to recover. I believe this applies to all Black folks. We should indeed choose liberation, which according to hooks (2005) means choosing "to heal" and "to love" (although this can be extremely hard for obvious reasons). This to her is the beginning of "authentic activism" (p. xxx). Feelings would expect this from all our youths.

Chapter Nine
African Sites of Memory in African-American Children's Literature

As we advance into the twenty-first century Africa remains a mystery to many in our global community. For some, it is still a continent plagued by disease and famine. For others, like our Black brothers and sisters in the diaspora, it holds the key to who they are, and what they are capable of accomplishing.

Although not all Blacks in the diaspora would agree that Africa is important in their quest for individual and group identity, there remains a handful that feels that Africa is indeed the answer. Among this group are some authors of children's books, who believe that integrating African sites of memory in stories or poems can help Black children to not only develop a positive self-image but be able to also survive the White Western culture better. Such sites would trigger memory of life as it was for Black people long before their ancestors were forcefully brought to the New World. Thus the stories that evoke such sites would expose these children to the different accomplishments of their African ancestors and the different survival strategies that had sustained Black people for centuries.

Cultural critic Cornelius Holtorf (2002) citing Marquard explains that sites of memory "exist to help us recall the past—which is perhaps necessary in order to make living in the modern world meaningful" (unpaged). Such sites can embody specific objects, works of art, special artifacts, and special individuals. In addition, Paul Connerton (1989) adds that "two acts of transfer" that help people to remember the past are "commemorative ceremonies and bodily practices" (p. 40). What the prominent African-American authors whose works I will discuss in this chapter have done is write stories or poems for children that include special rituals and significant artifacts from Africa.

Those who integrate African sites of memory make references to cultural practices found in specific African villages and towns in the distant past; some make references to African art, and to Africans with special powers. Regardless of the geographical location, or the cultural references made in such stories, each author succeeds in forging a link between experiences of Blacks in the diaspora with those of Blacks in Africa.

Many may wonder why these authors take the trouble to integrate African sites of memory in their works. Although I had touched on this briefly in my discussion of images in Chapter 1, I still find it necessary to discuss specific images of Africa (or what I prefer to refer to in this chapter as sites of memory) that are prevalent in children's books written by African-Americans. I would also like to *fully* understand how and why these artifacts are significant to a group of people who have been separated from the African continent for centuries. I would begin by acknowledging that cultural critic Dixon (1994) believes such sites of memory help "in the construction of a viable African-American culture" (p. 18). Thus, it is one way African-Americans in the New World can maintain the link between their African ancestry and their present reality as Americans.

This culture of remembering is important to every group of people—for Blacks in the diaspora even more so because of their social reality as marginalized people. Memory becomes a useful tool in people's daily survival as individuals and as a group. Dixon (1994) gives us a specific example of how well memory can serve us. He remarks that, when one is " lost in upper Manhattan," to "reorient" oneself requires that one "remember[s] the people who lived there and those who continue to live there." It is the only way one is going to find his/her "directions" back home (p. 20). The six authors whose works I have included here have attempted to do just that. They have tried to provide literary road maps for Black children to "reorient" themselves as they remember their African heritage. In so doing, these children may tap into cultural memory defined by Cornelius Holtorf (2002) as " the collective understandings or constructions of the distant past." This cultural memory may make it possible for them to recognize subtle markers of injustice and to learn effective strategies that would enable them to handle such social injustices with courage and tact.

Within this generic category of cultural memory, the six authors evoke specific sites of ancestral, artistic, spiritual, and genetic memory. I will discuss a total of nine books. I focused on these writers in particular because not only are they well known, but they have also won major awards. Some of them write primarily poetry; others write both fiction and poetry for children. Although I have included a book by Lucille Clifton and another by Kwame Dawes, I have hesitated to note that the chapter will focus on eight authors. This is because the primary reason for adding the two books in question is because of the illustrators John Steptoe and Tom Feelings, who are also authors in their own right. After reading all nine books I identified four major African sites of memory:

1. African sites of ancestral memory
2. African sites of artistic memory
3. African sites of spiritual memory
4. African sites of genetic memory.

African Sites of Ancestral Memory

Eloise Greenfield, John Steptoe, Tom Feelings, and Nikki Giovanni evoke African sites of ancestral memory in their poems or picture storybooks about Black experiences in the diaspora. This memory aims to reinforce African-American children's sense of cultural identity and sense of "selves." In such poems or stories, the child character becomes part of a real or imagined African community, and is able to appreciate his/her cultural heritage more. The child characters in these books learn very quickly that they are loved by members of their families and by members of their Black communities. The literary works that explore ancestral memory dwell extensively on African cultural traditions. In these works, the authors show the benefit of adhering to these customs, as they also insist that Black children should be proud of their African heritage. These writers have each made a deliberate effort to connect Black child readers in the diaspora with their ancestral African past.

In Greenfield's (1977) *Africa Dream*, a little girl dreams about Africa of long ago as she seeks to be part of the culture of her ancestors. This girl "went to the city / And shopped in the marketplace / For pearls and perfume," and "With magic eyes," she could "read strange words / In old books / And understood" (unpaged). She also "went to the village / And stood lonesome-still / Till my long ago granddaddy / With my daddy's face / Stretched out his arms / And welcomed me home" (unpaged). The girl participates in the communal festivities with her African relatives and friends. Later, she "turned into a baby / And my long-ago grandma / With Mama's face / Held me in her arms / And rocked me / Rocked me / To sleep" (unpaged). Therefore, the young girl is able to get a balanced view of what Africa is, and who Africans are. Africa is the home of her ancestors, a place where she can escape to momentarily whenever she needs comfort. It then becomes a home Greenfield's character believes would always welcome her regardless of the passage of time. In Africa she feels love, happiness, and a sense of security. Becoming a part of a community that has long-standing traditions makes her safe. In short verses Greenfield captures Africa's contributions to world civilization, reminding children of the continent's great history. The black and white illustrations are beautiful and dreamy as they depict the different emotions the child narrator feels throughout her imaginary journey.

The next two books that integrate African sites of ancestral memory are John Steptoe's *Birthday* (1972) and Lucille Clifton's *All Us Come Cross the Water* (1973) illustrated by Steptoe. While Greenfield takes readers on an imaginary journey to Africa, Steptoe and Clifton re-create Africa in the United States. One feature that stands out in both books is the fact that the child protagonists have African names. The families in the two books seem to have embraced traditional African village customs.

In *Birthday*, Steptoe explores community life in a neighborhood in the United States called the nation of Yoruba. In this fictitious community everybody works for the benefit of the other. Hence Javaka's eighth birthday has to be celebrated by all. As Javaka remarks, "We live right outside the brand new town of Yoruba. My Daddy and his friends have farms around it. Yoruba is the name of a nation of people in Africa and my daddy and his friends decided to name our place it" (unpaged). Members of this community try to re-create the memory of what it was like to live in a Yoruba village. Most of the characters have African names; so do the stores in their neighborhood.

As is common in most West African villages, the birthday celebration becomes a community event with other women helping Javaka's mother cook, while the fathers are working on the farms. This festivity is celebrated with African music, with the men playing "steel drums and bongos and horns" (unpaged). True to the Yoruba customs, the characters also "gave thanks for the health of the first-born of Yoruba . . . Javaka Shatu" (unpaged). The illustrations depict characters in African attire with the women dressed in wrappers and headscarves and the men sporting Afros, the style that reflects the 1970s setting.

Steptoe creates Black characters who are striving to live as best they can, and who do not hesitate to appropriate symbols from their African past to give meaning to their present. They do not also mind establishing a West African community within their new setting as they seek to carve out their own space from which they can uphold Yoruba cultural values. In spite of the geographical distance from Africa, they are determined to hang on to the cultural practices of their ancestors.

Lucille Clifton's *All Us Come Cross the Water* illustrated by John Steptoe is another story that depicts a family that has embraced traditional African culture, although not as extensively as in *Birthday*. The primary focus here is on the message that Black children should not be ashamed of their cultural heritage. In the story, Ujamaa is not confident enough initially to explain during a Social Studies lesson where his ancestors originate. However, understanding quickly that this may communicate the wrong message about his attitude toward his African heritage to his peers, he quickly learns more about his ancestors from his maternal great, great grandmother. Now he knows that his maternal ancestors hail from Whydah, Dahomey (now called Benin), and his paternal ancestors come from Ghana. This new sense of identity helps him to reclaim his voice in class, and for the first time he is able to tell the teacher who has been calling him "Jim" that his name is indeed "Ujamaa!" This cultural memory of Ujamaa's ancestry not only rekindles a new sense of self, but also makes him a role model for the other Black "brothers" in the class.

Tom Feelings' *Soul Looks Back in Wonder* (1993) evokes a variety of cultural memories. Like the other books already discussed, the poems make references to African beauty, African customs, and African ancestors, as they address the different kinds of struggles facing Black youth in contemporary America. It is a great collection of thirteen poems by renowned African-American poets, celebrating Blackness/Africanness and what these represent. Each poem is accompanied by a poignant illustration that evokes mixed emotions. Three poems in this collection that overtly echo African sites of ancestral memory are

Walter Dean Myers' "History of My People," Rashidah Ismaili's "Africa You Are Beautiful," and Lucille Clifton's "Under The Rainbow."

Myers' poem itemizes specific aspects of African culture that Black youths should be proud of, for it reminds them gently of the need to build on the strong cultural foundation Africa has provided.

> They say that beyond the blues—moan
>   there is continuance . . .
> A reaching back and a forward surge
> A place where Black dreams swell consciousness
> Even as the Niger swells old seasons into new life. (unpaged)

Ismaili celebrates Africa's natural beauty, claiming Africa completely as his home, for

> I am bound to you
>   by the drum beat of
> my heart that pumps the
>   blood of my birthright
> and You are mine. (unpaged)

Clifton also celebrates Africa's beauty as she explains to her Black readers that her "long [gone] grandmothers" are "dreaming of [her]," at night under the rainbow (unpaged).

"For the masai warriors," a poem in Giovanni's collection, *Ego Tripping and Other Poems for Young People* (1993) also echoes African sites of ancestral memory. In this poem Giovanni dwells primarily on the heroic African past when African men were extremely brave and ruled great kingdoms. She is calling again on Black youths to recapture this spirit that is part of their African heritage. All they have to do is remember their "father's drum" and "the leopard's screech." They should remember that they can also "sprint across the grassy plain and make a nation for the gods where [they] could be the man" (p. 9). As is expected, the poem echoes the brave deeds of Africans who lived long ago, comparing them to gods to make a point about the physical, cultural, and spiritual capabilities of Black people. Like most poems in this collection, it is quite inspirational. Virginia Hamilton notes in the foreword that Giovanni "gives young people tools to help them prevail in an America that can be overpoweringly hostile and indifferent to them . . . [y]oung people are taught how to live to know, and to remember who they are. There's deliverance for them in these poems of struggle and liberation" (p. x–xi).

In these stories and poems the writers long for their African ancestors; the children cherish the love they get from their African ancestors, their African-American families, and their new Black communities. Any child who reads these stories or poems may begin to understand the significance of adhering to a cultural heritage that has a potential to anchor Black people, so they do not lose their identities and "selves." For strength to face the daily challenges of modern life that is increasingly hostile to Blacks in the diaspora, these children need to remember the different strategies their African ancestors had used to survive similar experiences in the past. They also need to learn how to build strong African or Black communities that would sustain them in a capitalist and a highly politicized New World.

African Sites of Artistic Memory

Like Greenfield's *Africa Dream*, Margot Theis Raven's *Circle Unbroken* (2004) begins in America. In this story, the grandmother answers her granddaughter's question of how she came to sew. This takes us to an African village where the skill is learned and honed. In explaining, the grandmother tells a fascinating story of how her people managed to maintain their connection with Africa by preserving the basket-making tradition. It is a coming-of-age story, for it all began when grandfather was a boy and had to demonstrate that he was a man by weaving a basket. "They taught him to make the ropes and nets and traps; to hunt in the woods, and harrow and hoe; to make drums from logs to pound as he danced; and to sew great baskets to hold rice" (unpaged). He learned how to make a basket, "circle on circle, coil on coil" (unpaged). It was during this time that "the slave men came and bound him in chains and stole him from his village to a ship bound for a strange new land" (unpaged). The grandmother relates virtually the entire history of how African-Americans came to be in South Carolina, and how they survived the experience. While on the plantation, grandfather continued weaving baskets for:

> The grasses brought him comfort.
> His fingers knew their secret.
> "Never forget," they whispered,
> as he sewed palmetto strips
> in and out—around and through
> His circle grew and grew
> And when his fingers talked just right—
> his basket held the rain,
> and he remembered from where he came. (unpaged)

It is a powerful story of how a basket-making tradition is handed down from generation to generation to keep the memory of their African ancestry alive and to retain their unique identity in the New World. In essence, as Americans they came from Africa; as Africans they hailed from Sierra Leone, the region highly reputed for its basket-making skill, and they do take pride in this particular cultural heritage that sets them apart from other American Blacks. This tradition becomes the circle that ties these African-Americans to their African ancestors.

The grandmother explains further how the basket-weaving skill has continued to serve the Gullah people, and how it is a rite of passage that every child within their community must undergo.

> And time has come now, child,
> for you to learn the knot that ties us all together—
> The circle unbroken.
> And when your fingers talk just right
> that circle will go out and out again—
> Past slavery and freedom, old ways and new,
> and your basket will hold the past— (unpaged)

This may imply that regardless of the hardship brought upon the Gullah people by slavery, and the hardship they may continue to endure as a displaced group of people in the New World, their old tradition of basket weaving has helped them survive centuries of oppression. This artistic memory can never be taken away from them. Rather, it continues to bridge the gap between the young and the old, and the New World and the Old World.

Giovanni also integrates this site of memory in the title poem of her beautiful and inspirational collection of poems *Ego Tripping and Other Poems for young People* (1993). The collection itself celebrates African-American heritage as it points out challenges facing the youth in contemporary America as well. In "Ego Tripping," the title poem, Giovanni highlights different ways Africa has contributed to world civilization. This impressive legacy of hard work and tremendous success, she insinuates in the poem, should be built upon by the youth, whom she discourages from caving in to the insurmountable challenges they face daily in their new home. To her, they are capable of flying "like a bird in the sky." She creates limitless possibilities for African-American youths. All they need for motivation is a complete understanding of the historical accomplishments of their African ancestors—to know and appreciate the magnitude of their contributions to world civilization. "Ego-tripping" is virtually a "song of my African self." I strongly urge every Black child to read it:

ego-tripping

> I was born in the congo
> I walked to the fertile crescent and built the sphinx
> I designed a pyramid so tough that a star
>   that only glows every one hundred years falls
>   into the center giving divine perfect light
> . . .
> I sowed diamonds in my back yard
> My bowels deliver uranium
>   the filings from my fingernails are
>   semi-precious jewels

. . .
I am so perfect so divine so ethereal so surreal
I cannot be comprehended
   except by my permission

I mean . . . I . . . can fly like a bird in the sky . . . (pp. 3–5)

In these two works Raven and Giovanni show the necessity for children to remember what Africa has contributed in the ever-evolving world civilization. The story and poem also provide an opportunity for Black children to learn to recognize the different artistic skills their African-American ancestors had brought along from Africa to preserve their identity and to help them survive their new reality as enslaved people. These children should, therefore, be proud of their God-given talents and the artistic skills their ancestors have worked hard to sustain.

African Sites of Spiritual Memory

One of the oldest forms of spiritual memory found in books for children is the use of African magic. This is evident in the recurrent theme of the conjure man or woman in most tales of the supernatural. For example, in Charles Waddell Chestnut's 1899 collection of tales we read about different ways slaves use magic to resist White oppression. These conjure tales, that have been retold for children by several authors including William Miller, Kim Siegelson, and Patricia McKissack, continue to demonstrate the power of African magic. According to Mary Alice Kirkpatrick (2004), "conjure tales reveal moments of active black resistance to white oppression" (unpaged). The tales have been around for several centuries.

The children's book that explores African sites of spiritual memory is Virginia Hamilton's *The People Could Fly* (2004). She evokes African sites of spiritual memory by introducing the use of African magic in her folktale set on a slave plantation. Authors do this to show how enslaved Africans were able to use magic from the Old World to liberate themselves from the physical and psychological bondage of slavery. According to the editor's note, *The People Could Fly* is a "mythical old" tale, which has persisted over the years.

In the folktale, Hamilton captures how African-American characters use African magic to fly away from the hardship they face on the cotton fields. Initially when they are captured and brought into slavery:

"Say the people who could fly kept their power, although they shed their wings. They kept their secret magic in the land of slavery. They looked the same as the other people from Africa who had been coming over, who had dark skin. Say you couldn't tell anymore one who could fly from one who couldn't." (unpaged)

Slavery eventually stifles even those with the talent to fly. It almost breaks all the enslaved Africans' spirit, but Toby the man with the African magic would not let this happen. No longer willing to take the torture from their White masters, Toby says the magic chant and those who had the ability to fly regain it and fly "Way above the plantation, way over the slavery land. Say they flew away to *Freedom*" (unpaged). Hamilton notes that,

> "The People Could Fly" is a detailed fantasy tale of suffering, of magic power exerted against the so-called Master and his underlings. Finally, it is a powerful testament to the millions of slaves who never had the opportunity to "fly" away. They remained slaves, as did their children. (unpaged)

Although Black children reading this tale in the twenty-first century may not necessarily believe that people can actually fly or that there is African magic, this fantasy still has a potential to empower some readers. It may help them to realize that once one gives in to despair, it is hard to accomplish much. Rather, they would have to learn to search within themselves for that untapped inner strength or potential to enable them to overcome physical hardships and transcend emotional or psychological barriers that may prevent their bodies and spirits from flourishing. This African site of spiritual memory can be very effective and still has some relevance in today's society.

African Sites of Genetic Memory

The last site of memory I identified is what I refer to as genetic memory. I arrived at this terminology after watching the Sundance television documentary, *Motherland: A Genetic Journey* (2003). In this documentary, some Blacks in the diaspora are curious to know from their DNA what part of Africa their ancestors actually came from. Two Afro-British people succeed in tracing their roots back to the Kanuri people, and the Bikoi people of Equatorial Guinea respectively. They are able to establish a biological connection between themselves and the African relatives they meet, even though they are fully aware of the fact that for obvious reasons they are *different* people now! The two books that demonstrate this site of memory are Tom Feelings and Kwame Dawes' (2005) *I Saw Your Face*, and Virginia Hamilton's (1967) *Zeely*.

Feelings' picture book *I Saw Your Face*, which he co-wrote with Kwame Dawes, and which is published posthumously, emphasizes the biological connections that exist between Blacks in the diaspora and Africans. The verses run thus:

I saw your face in Benin
And in Ghana near Takoradi . . .
I saw that face in Kingston . . .

Cruising through Louisiana
Past a field of collard greens
There you were in your overalls
Your eyes still following me . . .
I saw you waiting for the Brixton bus
Late January in London Town
You closed your eyes and quietly dreamed
Of land, sea grapes, and sun. (unpaged)

Basically, all the Black folks in this picture book seem to share a physical resemblance and similar aspirations. They are always watching, dreaming, and wondering about each other. At times, they see their relatives' faces on one another. Tom Feelings and Kwame Dawes seem to suggest that we are connected by biology and culture in spite of our geographical locations. Nothing can take that away from us, for we will always remain spiritually and biologically connected!

In the foreword, Dawes notes:

One day, Tom Feelings and I were talking about his journeys around the world and he told me about all the faces that he saw in Africa that he had seen in New York, where he grew up, and Guyana, where he worked for years, and in the many places he had visited around the world where people of African descent live. (unpaged)

Noticing this resemblance among Black people across the globe motivated them to write this story.

Hamilton's *Zeely*, a realistic fiction, also echoes this genetic site of memory. In this story, Elizabeth Perry also known as Geeder fantasizes that Zeely, a mysterious young woman working with hogs on her uncle's farm, is an African queen or the descendant of an African queen. She becomes fascinated with this woman and watches her every move, especially after she finally finds a photograph of an African woman who looks like Zeely. Hamilton explores this theme of biological connections in a delicate manner as she demonstrates that there is a possibility that Zeely could be related to the woman in the picture, but sometimes it is hard to really know.

Although Geeder eventually learns from Zeely that it is all in her imagination, readers learn nonetheless that there is a biological link between Blacks in the diaspora and Africans. That element of mystery about African-Americans' African lineage continues to exist. Hamilton writes:

Geeder had found something extraordinary, a photograph of an African woman of royal birth. She was a Mututsi. She belonged to the Batutsi tribe. . . . Except for the tribal gown the girl wore and the royal headband wound tightly around her head, she could have been Zeely Tayber standing tall and serene in Uncle Ross' west field. (p. 49)

As Blacks in the diaspora use their DNA to trace their genetic roots, more and more would be able to locate the specific region in Africa where their ancestors came from. For African-American writers of children's books this may mean that instead of using generic Africa as a setting in their stories, they can now conveniently select a specific country that ties them back to their roots.

African sites of memory in the stories or poems discussed in this chapter, I have finally concluded, are to help displaced Blacks to move forward. There was a time when it served only African-Americans; however, these sites of memory have become powerful points of cultural reference even for African immigrants who by choice or circumstance are unable to physically return to their homeland as well. As Black children in the diaspora attempt to "reorient" themselves in a new world that renders them invisible, and that pits them against one another, these African sites of memory can perhaps ease their pain. Thus, these children may have "to engage into the past . . . to deal with it . . . 'if [they] are going to shape a future'" with them as key players (Paule Marshall, as quoted by Feelings in *The Middle Passage*, 1995). They may also have to keep honing and refining their survival skills to suit their present-day reality.

It is hard to tell whether these African sites of memory in children's books are actually helping or can help Black children without carrying out a systematic study. However, it is always a good idea to expose children to their cultural heritage. Whether it makes a difference to them at the time or not, we know that it is only a matter of time before they would start seeking answers about their racial and cultural identities that position them as inferior others in our global community. These stories would always come in handy then. Constructing sites of memories does not only demand courage because one needs to first acknowledge that there is something about society that is disorienting Black children, and then to seek realistic ways to begin to reorient them. Of course, literature is only one tool that can be used to accomplish this. For now let us continue to use it to serve our goal of creating possibilities for all children.

I must also comment that although romanticizing the past can be problematic, as I pointed out in Chapter 1, perhaps someone still needs to remind us of such glories and bravery. However, we should still be wary of the fact that the African past like others was not always as glamorous as some of the stories have made them out to be. Our biggest challenge, however, continues to be how we can get our children to see their ancestral land as a source of healing as they confront the daily experiences of social injustice in the New World. It is a challenge because all they see in the media is a continent that either continues to solicit aid from the West or continues to destroy itself with weapons negotiated, borrowed, stolen, bought, or received from the West. Authors, therefore, should attempt to integrate survival strategies into their literary works that are more relevant to Black children living in contemporary societies. I am aware of the fact that it is not my place to dictate to an author what he/she should focus on in a story or poem. However, I believe that this is a worthy goal we should strive to accomplish, for indeed there is a major gap in our storytelling discourse waiting to be filled! And until this happens our children have just stories about our heroic past to contend with, but no future to look forward to.

Afterword

Unless our community becomes "self-sustaining" it is hard for our literature to "circumvent . . . white images [that] are implanted at the core of black life . . . We still at times are not sure as to how much of our image is us; to what extent we are the sole authors of our myth, our peoplehood."

(Carolyn Gerald, 1969)

Chapter Ten

When Illustrations by Africans Lack Visual Appeal, How Should African Readers React?

In his 1995 publication, Osa claims that African children's literature is no longer a neglected genre. In the same introduction he cites different ways people have attempted to disseminate information about African children's literature. He also points out that critics for this category of literature are rare, and hopes that many more will develop an interest in it as scholars continue to engage in critical discussions about African literature in general.

Although critics of African children's literature are no longer as "rare" as Osa claims, there continues to be a dearth of African writers and illustrators of children's books. This inadvertently means that a majority of the images of Africa depicted in children's books (as I have already mentioned in an earlier chapter), especially picture books that are crucial to children's early literacy development, are produced by Westerners or African professionals residing in developed countries.[1]

This trend may communicate different messages to African children about their "selfhood" and continent. One obvious message is that reading about African cultures is not important. Consequently, it does not really matter whether the literacy curriculum in most African schools is driven by textbooks packed with excerpts from Western classics, or excerpts from some African folktales that contain stereotypes and trite vocabulary. Having been exposed to this narrow view of their world in textbooks, some of these children can begin to accept the fact that their culture lacks substance. Not having access to a variety of books that depict African children's experiences may force those whose parents are affluent to order *real children's books* from the West. Most often these books focus primarily on White children's experiences. African children who belong to this privileged class may in turn read these books with great "hunger," innocently consuming some of the racist messages that could be embedded in the different stories, which supposedly are meant to entertain and educate all children. The outcome of such encounters, however, is the subsequent reinforcement of the belief in the ideology of Africans' inferiority vis-à-vis White, Western supremacy.

Renowned African authors of literature for adults infuriated by this neglect have attempted to fill in the gap in different ways. For Flora Nwapa the thought of having Nigerian children reading the racist imported stories that were prevalent when she was growing up was too much.[2] So, she took on the task of not only writing but also publishing books for children. This gesture, as well intentioned as it was, was not without its own challenges. There were issues she had to contend with. Besides the question of cost, which most publishers of books about Africa would identify as a major factor, she had to worry about the distribution of these books to rural and urban communities—both of which have distinct cultures in terms of class and ethnicity! Above all, she also had great difficulties finding affordable qualified artists who were willing to illustrate books for children. For Nwapa, "the greatest problem in writing for children is related to the illustrations," for illustrators are not only "rare" in Nigeria but also "seem incapable of capturing children's faces" (p. 269).[3] One of her picture books, which she believes is well illustrated, is *Mammywater*. However, because it was so expensive to produce the bright colors that made the book visually appealing to children, she was unable to break even financially.

Most scholars of children's literature about Africa are concerned about this. We are fully aware of the disparity that continues to exist among the illustrations done by Western illustrators that depict African children's experiences in books and those done by our brothers and sisters in the continent. For the most part this is because illustrating children's books can be an expensive process. But like Nwapa we also have to contend with the lack of adequately trained professionals in our local communities. The question then is: should we continue to allow Western artists to be the primary illustrators of children's books about Africa, since their pictorial depictions have more aesthetic and visual appeal? Or should we encourage African artists with skills not yet fine-tuned to participate in defining our culture visually in children's books? This is tough. In rejecting books illustrated by these Africans because of their quality, we may inadvertently be aiding and abetting colonial images that may communicate negative messages about Africa and Africans in books illustrated by Westerners, and most probably by former Peace Corps members.[4] Given some of the concerns raised by Nwapa, how are we sure that African illustrators themselves may not perpetuate stereotypes about their people, since they are products of a colonial educational system?

Even though the latter is possible, I argue in this chapter, like Veronique Tadjo (2005), that we should take our chances with African illustrators. The racist and stereotypical images of Africa are still prevalent in books without them as active participants. Although I understand that such images coming from Africans themselves can be more damaging, I believe that with the appropriate professional training, budding African illustrators can eventually transcend these colonized and what some have described as "amateurish" depictions of their own people and culture.[5] I am also aware of the fact that because of the African elite obsession with being perceived as intelligent as their Western peers, tolerating anything less than the established Western literary ideal may seem like lowering the standards.[6] This notwithstanding, I do not think we should quickly dismiss these struggling illustrators and promote only books with better-quality illustrations from the West. Encouraging African illustrators would boost their self-esteem and perhaps help them to begin to perceive themselves as serious professionals—a first step toward accomplishing excellence. As they take advantage of professional development opportunities now being offered by international organizations or by their local governments in different parts of Africa, not only will they be able to eventually produce better-quality illustrations, but they may also be able to represent Africa in ways that are uplifting to our children. Hopefully, with more of them in the field, colonial and neocolonial images of Africa and Africans that are currently prevalent in picture books may gradually begin to disappear.

Mabel Segun understands the magnitude of the problem. Her biggest concern revolves around "a dearth of good authors," and the fact that there is "a scarcity of trained children's book illustrators." She also acknowledges that "the inhibiting economics of publishing in four colours and a general lack of awareness of the importance of illustrations in children's books" further complicate the issue (p. 77). Although she sounds disappointed and frustrated in the article, she still believes that the situation can be remedied partly because Africa *really* does have some award-winning illustrators with international recognition.[7]

On the issue of cost, she suggests that publishers could encourage African illustrators to use two, instead of four colors for books that target the younger children, and pencils, pens, and ink for older children. She believes that the success of illustrations "depends on the cultural relevance, thematic suitability, fluidity and most on the image" (p. 88). To illustrate this point, she compares an earlier version of an illustration of her autobiography *My Mother's Daughter* set in the 1930s and 1940s to a revised version—both done in black ink. The point of the comparison is to show how beautiful pictures can be created with minimal materials, paying attention to the cultural context, social class of the subject, and the historical context. In a sense, she provides African publishers and illustrators with options on how to work with a limited budget to produce quality picture books for all African children, rather than forget about them completely, or let children from middle-class homes whose parents can afford books from the West continue to consume the imported images (good or bad) of Africa.

African and Western Visual Interpretations of Africa: An Analysis of Eight Picture Books

To demonstrate the gravity of the picture book situation in Africa, it is necessary to compare visual images of Africa from African and Western perspectives. I have selected four books that reflect contemporary Africa from an African perspective: Meshack Asare's *Meliga's Day* (2000) and *Sosu's Call* (2002), Njeng's *Vacation in the Village* (1999), and Bognomo's *Madoulina: A Girl Who Wanted to Go to School* (1999). These picture books are written and illustrated by Africans. Asare's picture books have received critical acclaim from scholars abroad and in Africa. *Sosu's Call*, which is set in contemporary Ghana, won the 1999 UNESCO award for tolerance and was an Africana 2003 honor book. Njeng and Bognomo are relatively new authors/illustrators in the field of children's book publishing. However, Njeng's *Vacation in the Village* is an Africana 2000 honor book.[8]

To match these books I have also selected four books illustrated by Westerners (Europeans and Americans) set in Ghana, and Cameroon. These include Knight's award-winning *Africa is Not a Country* (2000), Gail E. Haley's *A Story, A Story* (1970), Oyono's *Gollo and the Lion* (1995), and Tchana and Pami's *Oh, No, Toto!* (1997).

When we compare these two sets of books by Africans and Westerners, undoubtedly we can tell that those illustrated by Westerners have better visual appeal, and thus have a greater chance of grabbing any child's attention more so than the ones done by Africans. Asare's *Meliga's Day* is a wonderful picture book that describes all the things Meliga notices on the way as he rushes home from school, to take care of his animals in the field. The watercolor illustrations are captivating and are quite expressive. The story text that accompanies the illustrations is also interesting. It is a story many children from rural communities in the north can relate to. Unlike *Meliga's Day*, Asare's *Sosu's Call* addresses a pertinent social issue that exists in most West African countries—the discrimination against people with disabilities.

In the July–August 2002 *Black Issues Book Review*, Sonya Kimble-Ellis describes *Sosu's Call* as a

> beautifully illustrated text [which] comes to life with subtly blended water-colors and brushed images that wonderfully reflect the author's African influence. [Asare's] use of color illustrates the mood of the story. The muted tan washes at the beginning of the book convey the child's despair. The brighter hues by the tale's end illustrate Sosu's happier circumstances.

I agree with this view; however, I also feel that although the illustrations are powerful, they lack the glitter or glow that could hold the child reader steadfast to it. The message of the book is what may keep him or her, for Asare succeeds in drawing attention to Ghanians' attitude toward people with disabilities. Done in soft watercolors that may seem dull at times, he captures the mood of the story and does succeed in representing a certain aspect of Ghanaian culture realistically. This picture book has been so well received that it was identified as one of twelve of "Africa's finest books of the 20th century."[9]

Knight's *Africa is Not a Country* is an informational book on the different countries that exist in Africa. The illustrations done by O'Brien are bright and beautiful to look at. They portray African children in a positive light as we read about their daily activities in the different countries (urban or rural) in which they reside. In the section that deals with Ghana, she paints the picture of two beautiful children in a classroom as they listen attentively to the lesson being taught. It may be unfair to compare what Asare tries to accomplish in *Sosu's Call* with what O'Brien does in *Africa is not a Country* because they capture different moods and focus on children in different situations, and who belong in different social classes. Thus while one evokes admiration, pity, and empathy for a handicapped boy who is being discriminated against by his family and community, the other evokes only admiration and respect for the determined African girls in school uniforms learning about their culture.

Haley's Caldecott award-winning book, *A Story, A Story*, is packed with exquisite illustrations. Compared to *Meliga's Day*, they seem more fascinating to me. Her images appear to be lifelike with the vibrant colors holding the reader's attention consistently throughout. This notwithstanding, I would hesitate to say her illustrations are absolutely better than those found in *Meliga's Day*, which I find intriguing and more eye-catching than the ones in *Sosu's Call*. Rather, I would attribute the differences more to their distinct artistic styles.

When we compare O'Brien's illustrations of Cameroonian children in Knight's book, we notice clearly that they are aesthetically superior to those depicted by Njeng in *Vacation in the Village* and Bognomo in *Madoulina*. In O'Brien's illustrations we notice dignified children, even though we can tell right away that they are not materially well-off. We do not pity them; they are depicted as ordinary human beings going about their daily business. Njeng's illustrations in *Vacation in the Village*, like Bognomo's, are not as professionally done as O'Brien's in *Africa is Not a Country*, or as Corvaissier's in Oyono's *Gollo and the Lion*.[10] It is not a question of color because the pictures are bright. It is more a problem with mastery of the art or specific techniques. Some critics have described them as "simple" and "amateurish."[11] Although done in bright colors, the children's features are not clearly defined. At times, it is hard to tell the difference between a girl and a boy from their facial features. One is able to do so mainly from their attires, which tend to be gender specific—girls in dresses and boys in shorts or trousers. Carol Raker Collins (2000), a reviewer for Africana Children's Book award, remarks that "[t]he lighter, brighter colors are effective, but the darker colors, especially when superimposed on a dark background, lack clarity and make the figures difficult to see."

Bognomo's *Madoulina: A Girl Who Wanted to Go to School* has the same problems. In fact, most reviews for this picture book are so harsh that I feel they border on cruelty. *The Horn Book Guide* notes that "[t]he simple declarative text, though choppy, gives a good idea of what some girls face growing up in many developing countries, but the illustrations which awkwardly rendered human figures are amateurish" (Horn Book Guide Online). Diane S. Marton, a librarian at Arlington County library, Virginia, dismisses it as a "poorly executed adaptation."[12] According to *Kirkus Review* (1999), "the bright, folksy illustration is unusually naïve." Only one reviewer, Maggie Canvin (2000), claims that Bognomo's book is attractive. It also helps to know that she reviewed this for H-Afrteach. Her review, although well intentioned, at times seems condescending.

Regarding Njeng's *Vacation in the Village*, Diane S. Marton notes that "the bright childlike illustrations are equally unappealing" (barnesandnoble.com). Njeng's picture book, however, got a much more sympathetic and inspiring review from Donnarae MacCann (2000), a renowned Africanist scholar who understands the challenges these African illustrators face. She notes,

> Njeng uses a palette of rich colors and paints bold and delicate shapes as a means of producing the warmth and solidarity of his theme. Using this pictorial technique, he highlights body language rather than facial detail.

Although MacCann's review sounds empowering, I cannot help but wonder about Njeng not being able to depict the characters' facial features in a clearly distinctive manner.

When compared to another picture book set in Cameroon, Njeng and Bognomo's still lag behind. Tchana and Pami's *Oh, No, Toto!* (1997), set in northern Cameroon, is also better illustrated. The illustrations by Bootman, a man originally from Trinidad, are splendid. Like O'Brien's, the reader is drawn to the images because one can tell the differences that exist among the characters, and one can identify their distinct mannerisms that add to the humor in the story. The illustrations are professionally done and are as colorful as O'Brien's as they accompany the story of Toto Gourmand, a child who eats too much.

Although the stories in Njeng and Bognomo's books have good messages to communicate about Cameroonian children, this may not be achieved if the child reader is unable to get past the illustrations. However, with better images children are easily attracted to a picture book. In the course of reading or admiring the beautiful illustrations they may actually want to find out what the author is saying in the print text, as my sons responded to Trina Schart Hyman's illustration to Alexander's (1997) *The Fortune-Tellers* several years ago just after it came out. It is an experience I will always relish.

When my children first saw the picture book their immediate reaction was, "What kind of book is this?" Yenik, my then seven-year-old son, began twisting his nose in disgust, then suddenly burst out, "Oh, it's Africa people!" This aroused their curiosity. Luma, the second son (age six), grabbed the book quickly and began leafing through its pages. "No," he protested, "It's Cameroon people!"

From the illustrations he was able to identify a specific group of people—his people—whose cultural experience he had actually participated in before coming to the United States.

The beautiful people, facial expressions, colorful clothing, calabash bowls, well-carved wooden furniture, and tropical village setting all helped to bring my country of origin alive in the pages of Alexander's and Hyman's picture book and gave me a nostalgic feeling. Hyman portrayed the people of northern Cameroon with great care, capturing little details that reflect her sensitivity toward the culture. However, there are places where the text presents details of situations that are not typical of the Cameroonian cultural experience. The illustrations, however, remain true to her text. The scene where the lion chases the older fortune-teller, even though it conforms to the text, can cause tension. To the average Cameroonian, it shows complete lack of respect for the elderly! Showing Cameroonians sharing space with monkeys can also create tension, as I discussed at length in Chapter 2.

There's an acute need, then, for Africa to train good illustrators who are more familiar with the region and local culture, as Segun and Nwapa have suggested. Like Segun, I hope we encourage budding artists such as Njeng and Bognomo, and support experienced and award-winning professionals like Asare, Veronique Tadjo, Baba Diakite, Claire Mobio and others to continue representing our cultural experiences in picture books. Although I did not examine Tadjo, Diakite, and Mobio's illustrations closely as I did Asare's in this chapter, they are equally as professionally well done. Tadjo and Diakite, for the most part, prefer folk art, which goes particularly well with their respective folktales, *Mamy Wata and the Monster* (1997), *The Hat Seller and the Monkeys* (1999), and *The Magic Gourd* (2003). Mobio's illustrations in Fatou Keita's *The Smile Stealer* (1996), however, is a blend of representational and expressionistic art. The highly entertaining story is packed-full with vibrant pictures that can sustain young children's attention for the duration of the story.

Dismissing African artists' works as amateurish would only make our children dependent on the West permanently and further strip us of our African dignity (Nyamnjoh, 2004). When this happens, anything is possible, for we will continue to have images that may not accurately represent us.

O'Brien and Bootman are just a few exceptions of Western illustrators who have depicted African children in positive lights. There are several already illustrating stories set in Africa or about Africa who unconsciously or consciously distort *our* culture, overlook significant cultural nuances, or depict Africans through a neocolonial lens. Donnarae MacCann and Yulisa Amadu Maddy (1996) have identified a series of picture books by Western authors and illustrators that demonstrate this. For example, although Vanessa French's illustrations in Virginia Kroll's *Africa: Brothers and Sisters* (1993) are beautiful, some of the information Kroll presents about Africa is inaccurate. Kroll and Roundtree's *An African Mother Goose* (1995) also perpetuates the stereotype of Africans sharing space with dangerous and exotic animals, despite the vibrant illustrations.[13] Even Barbara M. Joose's recent picture book, *Papa, Do You Love Me?* (2005), which is beautifully illustrated by Barbara Lavallee, continues to promote the stereotype of Africans as exotic beings.

All these distortions and/or stereotypes remind us of the urgency to participate in the book-making process, so that we do not remain "culturally dependent" on industrialized nations as Altbach predicts (1995, p. 488). Also, as Ekwensi suggests during an interview with Larson, writing should be "regarded . . . as a career" and not simply as a "charitable pursuit to educate and entertain readers with nothing coming to the writer" (Larson, 2001, p. 2).[14] Like Ekwensi, Kotei cannot forget the success of the Onitsha Market Literature, "which burst upon the Nigerian reading public in the 1950s" (Kotei, 1995, p. 480). He considers this as a "phenomenon of literary profusion without comparison anywhere in Africa, before or since" (p. 481), and poses the following question: "How can one account for the ability of Onitsha Market Literature to achieve success without any of the persons involved having received much training in writing, printing, publishing or book selling?" He believes this was as a result of what he terms "book hunger," for people were ready to read "any and all accessible material" (p. 481).

This continues to be true today when it comes to home videos produced for public consumption in the diaspora by Ghanaian and Nigerian entrepreneurs. Although the quality of most of these movies is not up to par with Hollywood standards, many Africans in the diaspora, myself included, "hunger" for these cultural images. They continue to be a phenomenal success, even though film critics and scholars would agree that the scripts are didactic, the acting spontaneous or forced at times, and the overall visual quality poor or at best average.[15] The bottom line is that Africans are watching and laughing, thinking and hoping for things to get better someday for them to eventually return home and participate in the culture they left behind on self- or forced exile. And, yes, the images have begun to improve!

It is necessary therefore for African writers and illustrators to produce books for their own children, even if initially the story texts and/or visual images may not be as aesthetically appealing as we may want. By stating this, however, I am not endorsing damaging images from irresponsible artists. We would have certainly accomplished a lot if one day, African children are able to find high-quality books in their towns and villages without necessarily depending on the goodwill of the relatives and/or friends abroad to send them books that depict African children's experiences through the perspectives of North American and European artists.

Chapter Eleven
Authenticity, Hybridity, and Literature about African Children

Children's literature, as many scholars and educators are aware, does not simply educate and entertain, but can also create possibilities for children. This is because images embedded in stories and illustrations can or do define reality for most children. For example, the early alphabet books about African-American children depict them as caricatures with exaggerated features. Eventually, as time changed and more African-Americans started telling their own stories, and as publishers became aware of what such images were actually conveying about Black people, these alphabet books were revised. As already mentioned in earlier chapters, images can suggest that a child's culture has or does not have any merit. They can also communicate the view that certain racial groups are superior to others. This image-making struggle will continue as writers and illustrators produce books for children. My concern now, though, is the plight of African children. Who will tell their stories? Who will capture their joys and pains in books *for them in particular* to read? Who will help them develop their own voices, so they can actually participate in the literary debate at the child level? I ask these questions because while most children in the West can take reading, books, and literature for granted, African children do not have this luxury. In Chapter 10, I provide some of the reasons for what I may loosely refer to as an African print literacy tragedy. In addition, if stories are written about African children, they are not really the targeted audience. Most often books that are published for them and about them locally may lack the aesthetic glow that glues children to books, or are just poorly produced with poor type-setting. The few books of higher quality are usually expensive, making it difficult for the average child to have access to it. With the public library system not functioning at all in most communities, children most certainly may not have the opportunity to have access to such books.

Africanist scholars continue to be bothered by this "literary barrenness" that is pervasive across continental Africa.[1] Some publishers in the West, aware of this acute need, have taken steps to address it in different ways. Boyds Mills Press, for example, has annual writers' workshops in the U.S. where they actually bring together professional and aspiring writers from different parts of the world to hone their skills and discuss publishing trends. The majority of the publishing houses in the United States have resorted to using already established Western writers to write about African children. Others such as Baobab Books in Zimbabwe encourage African writers and illustrators, whose works they publish and disseminate across Europe and at times locally in some African countries, to not give up. Still further, as Veronique Tadjo (2005) points out, "Les Nouvelles Editions Ivoiriennes's impressive production is expanding, attracting authors and illustrators from countries like Senegal, Mali, Togo, Benin, and Cameroon" (p. 20). This aggressive approach has produced some of the finest children's books about African children. Afrique Illustree also provides a forum where budding African artists hone their artistic skills in Belgium. Despite all these attempts, it is still extremely hard to publish what may be considered "authentic" literature for and about African children. Francis B. Nyamnjoh (2004) of the Council for the Development of Social Science Research in Africa (CODESRIA) has elaborated on this in his recent article.

Other scholars have postulated different theories. Some argue that because Africa is extremely diverse in terms of region, language, educational background, social class, ethnicity and so on, it would always be difficult to capture its multiple realities in children's books. Others contend that as long as these stories are written by Western authors, and published in the West the literature will never be authentic. Apparently, some publishers also share this view and have begun implementing what is known as co-production policies. This is a system which allows Western publishers to work closely with local African literary organizations to co-produce children's books about Africa. Boyds Mills Press did this with Aile Cameroun and the result was Bognomo's *Madoulina: A Girl Who Wanted to Go to School* (1999) and Njeng's *Vacation in the Village* (1999), picture books that have received at best but modest reviews.[2] Regardless, as Khorana (1994) notes, literature about African children, "like literature any-where in the world, is influenced by political, economic, and social conditions, philosophic ideologies, and the hopes and beliefs of the cultures that gave rise to it" (p. xiii).

Many may wonder why authenticity in literature about African children continues to be an issue, especially in an age of increasing mobility and global-ization. It remains an issue because Africans in general and their children in particular have been short-changed by this new reality. To understand how, all one needs to do is look at the subjects of most children's books set in Africa that are published in the United States.[3] In this concluding chapter, therefore, I want to identify and discuss critically some specific factors that have contributed or continue to contribute to the lack of "authenticity" in literature for children considered African. I also seek to explain why one could easily categorize this sub-genre of literature as a 'hybrid" one.[4] However, I must first acknowledge that the concept of cultural authenticity is not a new one, and as Freeman and Lehman (2001) have rightly observed, it is truly difficult to identify who really is a cultural insider! My argument as always is framed within the postcolonial theory, which I believe adequately describes the complexity of the cultural experience I attempt to examine here. According to Punter (2000), "the postcolonial is a field in which everything is contested, everything is contestable, from one's reading of a text to one's personal, cultural, racial, national stand-point, perspective and history" (p. 101). I believe this mirrors the predicament of literature about African children. Although I frame the discussion within postcolonial theory, I am also aware of the fact that most theories "were born in the western, Anglo Saxon world, and therefore can also be resented as inauthentic in their application to African literature" (Anyinefa, 2000, p. 7). In essence, that continues to be the case of literature about African children.

What exactly is African literature for children? Who exactly is writing this literature? And for whom? Why is it so necessary that we develop this sub-genre of literature? These are all questions that elude most Africanist scholars of children's literature. Knowing full well that African children can easily be forgotten, we make accommodations and accept any story about them. But we are also aware of the pitfalls, contradictions, and challenges involved in the process of creating books that depict what many may inadvertently believe to be African children's "authentic" experiences.

One of the first challenges I want to address is the question of the writer's background. As most scholars of children's literature have already observed, the bulk of literature about African children is published in the West and written by Western authors/illustrators. I have discussed this extensively in Part 1 of this book. Some of these artists write from experiences they had in specific African countries, some from extensive research, and others from stories heard from relatives and/or friends who have visited Africa. Their stories, whether rooted in cultural experiences directly lived or not, are suspect. For these stories to be considered authentic, as many authors who have done detailed research and visited the countries in question profess, one has to read them carefully to find out what is *authentic* in the characterization, setting, point of view, plot, themes, style, and overall cultural content.[5] Readers do not necessarily have to accept that a book is authentic simply because the author lived in the country. Freeman and Lehman (2001) demonstrated this complexity in their discussion of Abelove's *Go and Come Back* (1998), "a contemporary novel set in the Peruvian jungle village" (p. 38). They note that although the author had spent two years with the locals, it was still somehow difficult to capture an "authentic" experience, and the narrative "becomes a kind of metafiction about insider-outsider perspective" (p. 38). If I want to take this point further I would also say that even though I spent two weeks in May 2004 at Ife and Abuja, I do not believe that my understanding of the Yoruba culture during that short period will automatically make any children's stories I set in Ife or Illesha authentic. I would be wary of writers and illustrators who make such claims.

Dominant Image of Africa as Needy

A new trend is emerging now as non-profit organizations attempt to fill in the publishing vacuum as well. The dominant image of Africa in such books is one of *Africa and Africans as Needy*. Before I proceed, I must first commend these organizations for all their hard work and the endless services they render to Africa and Africans; however, as a scholar, it is my place to raise questions about their practices in regard to the publication of children's books. What exactly is more important as representatives from these organizations write books about African children: the African child, or the profit they intend to make from the book sales? I pose this question deliberately because of the popularity of a picture book that came out in 2002.

Although the stories these well-meaning NGOs tell can be touching as they evoke pity and sympathy for their African subjects, there are moments when these same stories seem to be objectifying African children. The reader may find him/herself wondering how the children in the story had survived before the particular NGO had actually begun rendering its services.

At a recent African Literature Association conference, Wangui wa Guru, an Africanist scholar, drew the audience's attention to McBrier's *Beatrice's Goat* (2001), a *New York Times* best-seller. She was touched by all the attention this picture book, sponsored by Heifer International (a charitable organization), had had so far. However, she was also concerned by the fact that "there was no dialogue of equality" in the story. As she rightly pointed out in her presentation, Beatrice is objectified throughout the story. Guru believes that even though it is a story about Beatrice, an African girl from Kisinga village in Uganda, the author does not include Beatrice's voice. Rather, Guru believes that McBrier insists on telling the story about an African girl who is able to go to school only after receiving a goat from "some kindhearted people from far away" (unpaged). This raises the age-old question of who has the right to speak for another; and if so, does it give the story more authenticity? I find Guru's analysis fascinating since I have also been following the success of this picture book for a while.

When a reader picks up the paperback version of *Beatrice's Goat* there's a red circle on the jacket cover that clearly states that, "buying this book helps needy families." At the bottom of that same cover are written the words: "New York Times Best-seller." Thus before one even begins to read Beatrice's story, one already has an image of an impoverished girl who must be helped. She is already an object to be rescued by Heifer International. Therefore, we may not really be reading to actually understand who this girl is; rather, because we feel sorry for her, we are looking for different ways the gift has improved the quality of her life in order to donate more money to Heifer International. Reading the story from this perspective already positions us as a "superior other," making us oblivious to the daily life in this village community, relationships between daughter and mother, sister and siblings, Beatrice and her peers, as we pity the protagonist for being so poor. Poverty then becomes an extremely bad thing African children should be ashamed of. The entire plot revolves around Beatrice's relationship with the goat. This is the story the Heifer International representative who had visited Kisinga village shares as a "cultural insider."

To confirm Guru's skepticism, a major article was written in the January 25 2004 edition of *New York Times* titled: "How a Goat Led a Girl Up the Path to Education" (p. 11). As was expected, it is a touching story about Beatrice Miira who "was immortalized in a best-selling children's book" (p. 11). Next to the article is a picture of the real Beatrice; below this is the picture book jacket cover of a much younger Beatrice with her goat. This article also dwells more on the role that Heifer International has played in making this young girl's dream of getting an education come true, reinforcing the content of the best-selling picture book. Beatrice is extremely grateful, but she is also fascinated with the fact that "Everyone I see is so rich . . . when I go to their homes, I see how rich they are"—meaning her benefactors (p. 11). Granted, this article is unavoidably good publicity for Heifer International which is doing a marvelous job in Africa, but does anyone really know how Beatrice truly feels? Does anyone in the organization care to know as they share her story with the rest of the world?

On Sunday, June 12, 2005 there was a follow-up presentation on *Beatrice's Goat*, this time on the prestigious news program *60 Minutes*. The journalist who interviewed Beatrice did not hesitate to condescend as he asked questions about her new life in the United States and her accomplishments. He remarked that nineteen-year-old Beatrice was basically straddling between "the African bush and New England" where she attends a prep school, and come to think of it, "it is a goat that sent her to school." He went on stating emphatically that at college, besides studying, Beatrice was also learning how to play tennis and finds the transition from life where they were always hungry to a new one of plenty "weird." The journalist, whom I found arrogant, concluded by reminding us that "sometimes all it takes is a goat to save a child."

During the report we see clips of young Beatrice sleeping on the same bed with her goat, and going everywhere with the goat. We later see nineteen-year-old Beatrice participating in the village festivities as they celebrate her return to "the African bush" she calls home. In less than thirty minutes the White male journalist succeeded in communicating how backward Africa is, and how animals are more capable of "saving" children than their human counterparts in this "African bush." Africans in Beatrice's communities should indeed be grateful to the twelve goats that will eventually "save" their children from poverty and illiteracy. This segment of news on *60 Minutes* is the ultimate objectification of Beatrice and her people. They are bush people who may have to depend on animals for their salvation. This becomes a powerful image for every African child who lives in a village, and who happens perchance to read the book. The journalist does not only succeed in flaunting his White, Western superiority but also manages to create a situation that could make Beatrice ashamed of the only home she has ever known. That home, as the journalist has declared to the perhaps millions of people watching the news program that evening, is "AN AFRICAN BUSH," a popular stereotype in children's books about Africa.

In *Playing the Races: Ethnic Caricature and American Realism*, Henry B. Wonham (2004) draws our attention to a similar plight faced by our brothers and sisters in the diaspora. Quoting Alice Walker, he remarks that "Caricatures and stereotypes of ethnic subjects, 'were really intended as prisons. Prisons without the traditional bars, but prisons of image'" (p. 4). If I use this same analogy with the African situation I am then forced to conclude that Africans have now been contained in the bushes where they really belong! A recent e-mail, which originated from Norbert Finzsch, a "German Scholar of African American History," and which has been circulating in different African listservs, confirms my view (as forwarded by Tarbinlam, 2005). In the e-mail Professor Finzsch expresses his concerns about an African village becoming part of a German zoo exhibit. Finzsch explains that,

> The way Africans and African Americans in Germany are perceived and discussed, the way they are present[ed] on billboards and in TV ads prove that the colonialist and racist gaze is still very much alive in Germany. . . . People of color are still seen as exotic objects (of desire), as basically dehumanized entities within the realm of animals. This also explains why a zoo has been selected as site for the exhibit.

Of course, many Africans were outraged and hence protested. Are we then no different from our animal neighbors confined in zoos for entertainment purposes? Is this Barbara Jantschke, the Director of the Augsburg Zoo's way of declaring officially that Africa is now one giant zoo and its people are animals that should be placed on display?

Reading this e-mail reminded me too much of Beatrice's situation. However, by focusing on her and the picture book about her, I do not mean to undermine the work Heifer International is doing in Africa. I am saying that they should be aware of the fact that these impoverished families they are helping are human beings too and deserve some amount of respect. It would only be fitting to spare them the embarrassment of announcing repeatedly that a goat saved their daughter.

Non-profit organizations that publish books about children can accomplish the same goal without necessarily objectifying their African protagonists. For example, in *Chanda's Secret*, Stratton (2004) weaves a beautiful and heartwarming story around Chanda, a fifteen-year-old southern African girl. Although he has an agenda to raise awareness about AIDS, he focuses on this girl's life and experiences. The reader participates in this girl's dilemma and struggles, and participates in the southern African culture, as he/she learns pertinent information about the killer disease. Chanda is not objectified; on the contrary, she is engaged in the entire process as she seeks ways to effectively address the health crisis within her community.

Pardon me for digressing. Now let us look at the next issue in the dialogue about authenticity in African literature for children—that of Africans living abroad who write stories set in Africa. Should readers consider these stories to be more authentic than others produced in the West? This is tricky, partly because this group of writers depends heavily on the memory of the Africa of their youth—what they had experienced as children and how they felt about this experience. One may argue that all authors of children's books suffer from this syndrome because they are not children themselves and in a sense cannot be considered "insiders." However, the situations seem to differ somewhat in that most Western writers do reside where their stories take place. Thus even though they are adults, they have the privilege of observing the daily experiences of their Western children with whom they share space. In the case of African authors who live abroad, unless they visit their respective communities constantly they are limited to memory of lived experiences and research. To some, then, the easiest compromise is to retell folktales they grew up with like Obinkaram Echewa does. Others, like Ifeoma Onyefulu set their stories in the village, communities they believe do not change as rapidly as urban centers, hence retain aspects of our past, cherished practices.[6]

Many authors of African literature for adults have acknowledged that stories set in the African past are wonderful; however, they encourage writers to also focus on the present.[7] To Achebe, it was necessary to do so before when African intellectuals felt the need to show the rest of the world that Africa had "culture, civilization, religion, and history" (Lindfors, 2002, p. 1). He does not believe that we need to prove our humanity anymore. Rather, like Soyinka and Tayan lo Liyong, he believes that African authors should focus on their present reality because "[a]s long as people are changing, their culture will be changing" as well (p. 1). It comes, then, as no surprise to hear that scholars have criticized Onyefulu for privileging the village over other settings and for depicting Africa as one big country.[8]

At this point in the discussion it would be easier to conclude that Africans residing in continental Africa are more predisposed to producing "authentic" literature for their children. Unfortunately, this is also problematic for several reasons, some of which I have discussed in Chapter 10. One major reason has to do with the fact that most of them tell their stories in colonial languages. This means they have to translate certain African expressions into the colonial language of their choice. When they do this, sections of the story may lose something in the translation process. This inadvertently compromises the quality and authenticity of their work, as is evident in Bognomo's *Madoulina*.[9]

Recently the colonial language that seems to guarantee a wider readership is English, as many African writers for children court the American audience with the purchasing power. Consequently, even reputable Francophone writers like Veronique Tadjo now prefer to switch colonial languages.[10] We cannot really fault them for doing this, if we rationalize the gesture as a survival strategy. However, I wonder how this move impacts on the quality and authenticity of children's literature written for and about African children. Punter (2000) also acknowledges that the use of English language "began as an imperial enterprise," which later became "a thoroughly commercial one" (p. 27). Thus many Africans may want to tell their stories in a language they feel comfortable with but the reality of the market forces or compels them to do otherwise. Charles R. Larson (2001) has identified this and other challenges African writers face.

During an interview with Lindfors (2002), Tayan lo Liyong also remarks that Western education has a great impact on how African writers tell their stories. Therefore, although they are expected to write from a supposedly insider's perspective, their consciousness has been shaped by Western colonial ideals and expectations. A side-effect of this colonial mentality, I would add, is Africans mimicking versions of simplified classics they had grown up with, especially children's books in the Lady Bird series. Besides this colonized mentality that may affect the authenticity and quality of literature being produced for and about our children, Tayan lo Liyong also asserts that the terrain is open mostly to Africans who can afford the right kind of colonial education and those who have access to publishers. This inadvertently means that many potential Africans with real storytelling talents do not have a chance. He gives an example of some of his childhood friends who had more talent than him but who could never hone their skills simply because they had limited financial resources and no formal education.

Despite all these reasons, many African writers of children's literature would agree that one of their greatest obstacles is having access to publishers. This is because the publishing industry, whether abroad or within the continent, especially in the twentieth and twenty-first centuries, is driven by profit. Therefore, while local publishers may publish only works by established authors, Western publishers whose targeted audience is Western children and their parents with purchasing power would rather publish books they believe will sell. In so doing, they inadvertently dictate what should be written and by whom, further complicating the issue at hand. When all is said and done, then, our children's literacy fate depends mostly on these publishers who help to create an atmosphere that may lead to the production of books that reflect the hybridity of African cultures, or books that conform to "Western norms and expectations," or that compromise our humanity (Nyamnjoh, 2004).

Why do I raise all these concerns, some may ask. I have done so not to discourage aspiring and professional writers of books for African children. Neither do I want to further frustrate educators as they make decisions about multicultural or international books to include in their curriculum. Rather, it is an attempt to understand the complexity of the issue we are dealing with and to draw our collective attention to the dismal state of literature for and about African children in the twenty-first century. In a 1969 interview with Lindfors, when asked why he never portrayed "black hearted villains" in his novels, Achebe explains succinctly that, "[t]hose who have the best intentions sometimes commit the worst crimes" and thus must be educated (Lindfors, 2002, p. 4). I would like to believe that writers and publishers of books about Africa mean well; however, we still need to educate them on this issue. It is only through some form of education that many can overcome their ignorance about Africa and Africans and stop objectifying them. Earlier in the interview Achebe had remarked that, "the African artist has been left far behind by the people who make culture, he must now hurry and catch up with them" (Lindfors, 2002, p. 1). Indeed, we have to run to catch up with the rest of the world and participate actively in the business of cultural production.

In May 2004 I had the privilege to visit Ife where I spent several hours looking for books about Nigerian children at the Obafemi Awolowo University bookstore. I was saddened, though, at the quality of books produced locally, but mostly at the fact that in the middle of some of these books were warning statements from the publishers about piracy. This experience reminded me of my 2000 trip to Cameroon where I had visited several bookstores in different parts of the country, desperately searching for children's books in English (being an Anglophone) about African children and Cameroonian children in particular. As frustrating as the experience was, I continue to hope that those of us in the business of nurturing children will not forget about African children living in Africa. Thus, we should really not lose sight of the fact that as materially deprived as some may be, they are all our children. Providing assistance to these African children does not necessarily mean we should objectify or humiliate them. Like their peers in the West, they deserve the best and we should strive to give them the best that our minds, hearts, and pockets can produce—and that is quality books for and about them that capture their multiple realities!

NOTES

Chapter 2

1. See Sharron L. McElmeel's *100 Most Popular Picture Book Authors and Illustrators* (2000).
2. See "The Authors", http://www.twbookmark.com/authors/60/1545.
3. Although she may think that it is a futile attempt, or that minorities tend to play into the hands of the powers that be, it is still worth probing into. Indeed, identity issues are very complex because as we interact with people of other cultures, or live within a particular culture for long, we gradually lose our so-called "cultural authentic" self that might have defined us as an Other to these people. Trinh Minh-ha (1998) captures this brilliantly when she observes that "[t]he moment the insider steps out from the inside she is no longer a mere insider. She necessarily looks in from the outside while also looking out from the inside. Not quite the other, she stands in that undetermined threshold place where she constantly drifts in and out. Undercutting the inside/outside opposition, her intervention is necessarily that of both not quite an insider and not quite an outsider" (p. 3).
4. According to Ned Alpers, "the larger forces that produced the demand for bonded labor" is absent as well (qtd. in Randolph, 2003, p. 66).
5. See the Dillons's 2004 interview transcript at the Scholastic web site.
6. See Stephen Belcher's (2002) review.
7. For example, Marc Aronson, then of Carus Publishing feels that when educators insist that authors be socially responsible this can be a form of censorship. We had a healthy debate on this issue at the 2003 NCTE conference in San Francisco, CA.

Chapter 4

1. I will focus only on traditional African religion and Christian religion in this chapter.
2. Mbiti (1989) opposes the use of the term "ancestral worship" to describe traditional African religion. He notes that, "to see [African religion] in terms of ancestor worship is to isolate a single element, which to some

societies is of little significance, and be blind to many other aspects of religion" (p. 9).

Chapter 6

1. See Williams-Garcia's novel (2004) where the characters identify this as a major issue associated with female genital mutilation.
2. See Virginia Dike's (2005) article for a list of books published in Nigeria by Nigerian authors on love and relationships.
3. For more information on Children's Africana Book Award (CABA) see http://www.africanstudies.org/asa_childbook.html or H-Afrteach website.
4. See BuchiEmechetaArchive, p. 5, http://www.fb10.uni-bremen.de/englisk/ kerkhoff/AfricanLit/Emecheta/EmechetaArchives.htm, date accessed January 6, 2006.

Chapter 7

1. See Achufusi's article, "Feminist Inclination of Flora Nwapa" (1994), and Abdel-Jaourd and Ward's articles in *Research in African Literature* (1996).
2. See the following novels: *So Long a Letter* by Mariama Ba, *The Bride Price* by Buchi Emecheta, *The Rape of Shavi* by Emecheta, and *Yoruba Girl Dancing* by R. Bedford. For more on this, also read Angelita Reyes' *Mothering Across Cultures* (2002), in which she uses an interview with Ba to demonstrate this author's position on the role females play in African communities. She notes that "Ba focuses on the spiritual being of mother-women who despite having undergone emotional crisis and humiliation, are able to reaffirm faith in themselves and their females through the daughters—the next generation" (p. 162). See also Aegerter's (2000) article on postcolonialism and womanism, as well as Barbara Christian's on Black feminism (2000).
3. By "multidimensional oppression," Bostic implies that besides gender issues, Black women must deal with race, class, colonialism, and other forms of oppression.
4. David Punter (2000) insinuates that postcolonialism disempowers even a village patriarch, as the reader sees in Dangaremgba's *Nervous Conditions*.
5. There are many different ethnic groups in northern and northeastern Nigeria across Borno state and Gongola state where the novel is set. Some of these include Kanuri, Shawa, Manga, Marghi, Bade, Shuwa Arab, Hausa, Fulani, Tiv, and Berri Berri. In the introduction, Dr. Stuart Brown of the Centre of West African Studies, University of Birmingham, explains that "[m]uch of the power of the novel grows from the finely observed re-creation of a culturally and religiously 'mixed' village, somewhere in northern Nigeria, in the late colonial period" (p. 8).

6. Aegerter remarks that when Tambudzai is with Nyasha, they realize the greatest happiness. As individuals, however, each suffers tremendously. This shows Dangaremgba's bias toward the communal approach to healing.

7. As the keynote speaker at the 1999 EAPSU conference that took place at Millersville University, Tate explained why it was necessary to resist oppression without becoming decentered. By this she meant that activists should not allow themselves to be emotionally and psychologically destabilized because the consequences can be disastrous.

8. Alkali explains this in her novel. By "cast offs" she simply means that items considered valuable in the village are perceived as junk in sophisticated environments like the Nigerian city that has embraced Western civilization.

9. See Achebe's *Home and Exile* (2000).

10. See Achebe's comment on the "psychology of the dispossessed" in *Home and Exile* (2000, p. 72).

11. Aegerter (2000), who refers to Tambudzai and Nyasha as "communal protagonists," remarks that "Dangaremgba demonstrates the womanist dialectic of individual and communal identity through her dual protagonists: Nyasha and Tambudzai are fully realized as individuals, but they reach their fullest happiness and fulfillment together. Their friendship signifies the importance of community to individual autonomy. Through this figuration of friendship in dual protagonists, Dangaremgba is able metaphorically to heal colonization's severance of rural and urban Africas" (pp. 70–71).

12. bell hooks's chapter "Holding My Sister's Hand" addresses this issue candidly (hooks, 1994, pp. 93–110). So does Valerie Smith's (1997) article on Black feminists.

13. For more information on womanism read Alice Walker's *In Search of Our Mother's Gardens* (1983).

14. See Aegerter's (2000) article.

15. Since the feminist movement began, many Black feminists have been ambivalent about its role in their lives. To some its primary focus is to serve White women who are being oppressed by their men and has little to do with the plight of Black women. This is because Black females must deal with other forms of oppression in addition to gender, the primary focus of feminist inquiry. Its effectiveness then becomes questionable, as some sisters have realized that even among feminist groups there are some staunch White women who continue to ignore their racist attitude toward their Black peers. To alleviate this problem, more and more Black females and women of color are turning to womanism, which they believe serves their needs in a much more holistic way than the feminist stance ever could. See Christian (2000, p. 147) as well. Gina Wisker addresses this issue thoroughly in *Post-colonial and African Women's Writing* (2000).

16. For more on this, read Bostic's article, "It's a Jazz Thang: Interdisciplinarity

and Critical Imagining in the Construction of a Womanist Theological Method" (1998).

17. See Kolawole's book, *Womanism and African Consciousness* (1997).
18. I use "we" here in reference to all adults who are willing to participate in the liberation project.

Chapter 10

1. Not many books for children about Africa are published annually. For exact figures contact University of Wisconsin children's literature Librarian Patricia Kuntz or Brenda Randolph of Africa Access.
2. A typical example is a popular cumulative tale titled, "See Me Lakayana with My Spear" found in *Oxford English for African Primary Schools*, used in most Anglophone schools in West Cameroon in the 1960s. Also see Nwapa's article, "Writing and Publishing for Children in Africa— A Personal Account" in Roaul Granqvist and Jurgen Martini (eds), *Preserving the Landscape of Imagination: Children's Literature in Africa* (1997).
3. See Chikwe's *Village Boys*, which came out in 2003. The illustrations in this book, although in black and white, are well done. This demonstrates that there are some African illustrators who are well skilled in the art of the picture book and do an excellent job.
4. This does not necessarily mean that all books illustrated by Westerners transmit negative messages about Africa. However, because of our past history with the West, readers need to be cautious. There are some Western authors and illustrators who have done justice to depicting African culture in picture books. See MacCann and Maddy's *African Images in Juvenile Literature* (1996).
5. "Amateurish" is the term that has been used to describe artwork by some African scholars. Tadjo (2005) has remarked that "working away from the influence of Western art schools and literary theories has also helped illustrators and authors [Francophones] to develop a distinctive African style" (p. 22). I would imagine, however, that some must have received some professional training locally in Africa to perfect their art.
6. See Nyamnjoh's article (2004), "Publish or Perish to Publish and Perish" for an elaborate discussion of this issue.
7. Tadjo (2005) also notes that during the 1999 Bologna Book Fair "more than thirty-four African illustrators displayed their work, with nineteen originating from French-Speaking Africa" (p. 22). Therefore, there exist illustrators of varying reputations or skill levels in Africa, even if they are not as many as African educators and scholars (especially those of us living in the West) would have liked.
8. See http://www.childrenslit.com and Africa Access review website.
9. For more on this see news.bbc.co.uk/1/low/entertainment/arts and pages

20–21 of *African Literature Association: ALA Bulletin,* 28 (3/4, Summer/ Fall) (2002). However, *The Horn Book Guide* rates Asare's book as "unacceptable". According to the reviewer, "[t]he plot is unbelievable, and the book's tone patronizes its disabled hero."

10. I decided to add Oyono's picture book to demonstrate that even stories written by Cameroonians, but illustrated by Westerners (in this case Corvaisser, a French artist) seem to have better illustrations. Corvaisser's may not be as wonderful as O'Brien's or Bootman's perhaps because of the artistic style he emphasizes, but it is far superior to Bognomo's in *Madoulina.*

11. See Carol Baker Collins's review at Barnesandnoble.com and the Horn Book Guide review (July–December 1999).

12. Diane S. Marton seems to review books for *School Library Journal* on a regular basis.

13. For more information on cultural distortion, see Maddy and MacCann's *African Images on Juvenile Literature.*

14. This comment was made during a 2001 interview with Larson. For more information about publishing in Africa (according to Ekwensi) read the complete interview (Larson, 2001).

15. See Gray's article "Nigeria On-Screen" (2003) in Washingtonpost.com.

Chapter 11

1. East African author Tayan lo Liyong coined this term in reference to the state of Africa when he began writing.

2. To understand more about co-productions, read Freeman and Lehman's *Global Perspectives* (2001). They have attached a list of publishers engaged in this practice or in the business of translating international books in Appendix C of their book.

3. See Yenika-Agbaw's "Images of West Africa in Children's Books: Revising Old Stereotypes with New Ones?", in Kathy Short and Dana Fox (eds), *Whose Story is It?: Cultural Authenticity in Children's Literature,* Urbana, Ill.: NCTE, 2003, pp. 231–246.

4. Some European scholars whom I met at a conference in Zurich in November 2004 have objected to my use of this term; however, I still feel my use is appropriate.

5. See Freeman and Lehman's *Global Perspectives* (2001), Chapter 3.

6. See Echewa's folktale, e.g. *The Ancestor Tree* and Onyefulu's books that are set in the village. Some examples are: *A is for Africa* and *Emeka's Gift.*

7. For more on this read Lindfors' *Africa Talks Back: Interviews with Anglophone African Authors* (2002).

8. See Gcina Mhlophe, "The 'Story' the Mother of Creativity: My Journey as a Children's Writer," in *Sankofa: A Journal of African Children's and Young Adult Literature* 2 (2003).

9. Bognomo's story text in *Madoulina* doesn't flow. It clearly reads like a bad translation of an otherwise authentic piece of literature for children.

10. She expressed her concern about this issue during a meet-the-author session at the 30th African Literature Association conference that took place at Madison, Wisconsin in April 2004. Also in a recent article, Tadjo (2005) notes that there are indeed some African countries such as Niger and Rwanda that are "also publishing in their national languages" (p. 18).

Bibliography

References

Abdel-Jaouad, Heidi. "Too Much in the Sun: Sons, Mothers, and Impossible Alliances in Francophone Maghrebian Writing." *Research in African Literature* 27.3 (1996): 15–33.

Achebe, C. "Colonialist Criticism." In B. Ashcroft, G. Griffiths, & H. Tiffin (eds.), *The Post-colonial Studies Reader*. New York: Routledge, 1995, 57–61.

——. *Home and Exile*. New York: Anchor, 2000.

——. "Named for Victoria, Queen of England." In B. Ashcroft, G. Griffith, & H. Tiffin (eds.), *The Postcolonial Studies Reader*. London: Routledge, 1992, 190–193.

——. *Things Fall Apart*. Portsmouth, NH: Heinemann, 1959.

Achufusi, I. "Feminist Inclination of Flora Nwapa." In *Critical Theory and African Literature Today*. Trenton, NJ: Africa World Press, 1994, 101–114.

Adam, I. & Tiffin, H. "Introduction." In I. Adam & H. Tiffin (eds.), *Past the Last Post: Theorizing Post-colonialism and Post-modernism*. Calgary, Canada: University of Calgary Press, 1990, vii–xvi.

Adichie, C. *Purple Hibiscus*. New York: Anchor Books, 2003.

Aegerter, Lindsay Pentolfe. "Southern Africa, Womanism and Postcoloniality: A Dialectal Approach." In D. Gover, J. Conteh-Morgan, & J. Bryce (eds.), *The Post-colonial Condition of African Literature*. Trenton, NJ: Africa World Press, 2000, 67–73.

Afolayan, M., Kuntz, P., & Naze, B. "Sub-Saharan Africa." In L. Miller-Lachmann (ed.), *Our Family, our Friends, our World: An Annotated Guide to Significant Multicultural Books for Children and Teenagers*. New Providence, NJ: R. R. Bowker, 1992, 417–443.

"Africa's 'Best Books' Revealed." BBC News Online: Entertainment: Arts. Thursday, February 28, 2002, 09:21 GMT. Accessed April 13, 2004.

Alkali, Zaynab. *The Stillborn*. London: Longman, 1989.

Altbach, P. "Literary Colonialism: Books in the Third World." In B. Ashcroft, G. Griffiths, & H. Tiffin (eds.), *The Post-colonial Studies Reader*. London: Routledge, 1995, 485–490.

Anyinefa, K. "Postcolonial, Postmodernity: In Henry Lope's Le Pleurer-Rire." In D. Gover, J. Cotch-Morgan, & J. Bryce (eds.), *The Post-colonial Condition of African Literature*. Trenton, NJ: Africa World Press, 2000, 5–22.

Appiah, K. *In My Father's House*. Oxford: Oxford University Press, 1992.

Asante, M. *Afrocentricity: The Theory of Social Change*. Buffalo, NY: Amulefi Publishing, 1980.

——. "Afrocentricity and Culture." In M. K. Asante & K. Asante-Welsh (eds.), *African Culture: The rhythms of unity*. Westport, CT: Greenwood, 1985, 3–12.

Ashcroft, B., Griffiths, G., & Tiffin, H. "General Introduction." In B. Ashcroft, G. Griffiths, & H. Tiffin (eds.), *The Post-colonial Studies Reader*. London: Routledge, 1995a, 1–4.

——. "Introduction." In B. Ashcroft, G. Griffiths, & H. Tiffin (eds.), *The Post-colonial Studies Reader*. London: Routledge, 1995b, 55–56.

——. *The Post-colonial Studies Reader*. London: Routledge, 1995c.

Ba, Mariama. *So Long a Letter*. Trans. Modupe Bode-Thomas. London: Heinemann, 1989.

Bader, Barbara. "American Picture Books from Max's Metaphorical Monster to Lilly's Purple Plastic Purse." *Horn Book Magazine* 74.2 (1998): 141–156.

——. "How the Little House Gave Ground: The Beginnings of Multiculturalism in a New, Black Children's Literature." *The Horn Book Magazine* 78.6 (2002): 657–673.

Banker, Denise. "Too Real for Fiction: Themes in Young Adult Literature." *The ALAN Review* 23.1 (Fall 1995), http://Scholar.lib.vt.edu/ejournals/ALAN/fall95/Banker.html. Accessed December, 12, 2004.

BBC News. "New Nigerian Leads in Torso Murder." At http://news.bbc.co.uk/go/pr/fr/-/1/hi/england/2824417.stm. 2003. Accessed June 20, 2005.

———. "Swazi Ritual Killing Warning." At http://newsvote.bbc.co.uk/mpapps/pagetools/print/news.bbc.co.uk/1/hi/world/africa/2956348.stm. 2003. Accessed June 20, 2005.

Becker, Stephen. *A Production of Occasions.* Producer: Helmut Fischer. Sundance Television Channel. 2004.

Belcher, Stephen. "Improbable Prequel to a Pilgrimage." H-Net Reviews in the Humanities and Social Sciences. At http://www.h-net.org/reviews/showrev.cgi?path=181971017244525. 2002.

Bell, Bernard. "Beloved: Womanist Neo-slave Narrative; or Multivocal Remembrances of Things Past." In Harold Bloom (ed.), *Modern Critical Interpretations: Beloved.* Philadelphia: Chelsea House Press, 1999, 57–68.

Bernabo, Lawrance M. "African Culture from A to Z with Exquisite Artwork." October 2002, amazon.com. Accessed May 14, 2004.

Bishop, R. "Tom Feelings and *The Middle Passage*." *The Horn Book Magazine* 72.4 (1996): 436–442.

Blight, David. "W. E. B. Du Bois and the Struggle for American Historical Memory." In Genevieve Fabre and Robert O'Meally (eds.), *History and Memory in African-American Culture.* New York: Oxford University Press, 1999, 45–71.

Booker, K. *The African Novel: An Introduction.* Portsmouth, NH: Heinemann, 1998.

Bostic, Joy. "It's a Jazz Thang: Interdisciplinarity and Critical Imagining In the Construction of a Womanist Theological Method." In Kate Conway-Turner, Suzanne Cherrin, Jessica Schiffman, & Kathleen Doherty Turkel (eds.), *Women's Studies in Transition.* Newark, DE: University of Delaware Press, 1998, 138–155.

Canvin, M. "Review of Joel Eboueme Bognomo, *Madoulina: A Girl Who Wanted to Go to School*." H-AfrTeach, H-Net Reviews, http://www.h-net.msu.edu/reviews/showrev.cgi?path=182999 62307930. 2000. Accessed April 10, 2004. Children's Africana Book Awards. At http://www.childrenslit.com. Accessed April 10, 2004.

Chinweizu, Onwuchekwa, J. & Madubuike, I. *Toward the decolonization of African literature, Vol. 1.* Washington, DC: Howard University Press, 1983.

Christian, Barbara. *Black Feminist Criticism: Perspectives on Black Women Writers.* New York: Pergamon Press, 2000.

Clarke, J. H. *Africans at the Crossroads: Notes for an African World Revolution.* Trenton, NJ: African World Press, 1991.

———. "Introduction: The Middle Passage." New York: Dial, 1995.

Clarke, John. "Sexuality." In Dominic Wyse (ed.), *Childhood Studies: An Introduction.* MA: Blackwell Publishing, 2004.

Collins, C. "Review of Pierre Yves Njeng, *Vacation in the Village: A Story from West Africa*." At http://www.children'slit.com/th_af-cabaawards_html. 2000. Accessed April 10, 2004.

Congo. Paramount Pictures. The Kennedy Marshall Production. 1995.

Connerton, Paul. *How Societies Remember.* New York: Cambridge University Press, 1989.

Conrad, J. *Heart of Darkness.* Third edition. New York: Norton and Company, 1988.

Cott, J. "Chinua Achebe: At the Crossroads." In *Pipers at the Gates of Dawn.* New York: McGraw Hill, 1983.

"Diane Dillon and Leo Dillon." In Anne Cummire (ed.), *Something About the Author, Facts and Pictures About Authors and Illustrators of Books for Young People.* Detroit: Gale, 1988, Vol. 51: 47–64.

Diawara, M. "Afro-Kitch." In G. Dent (ed.), *Black Popular Culture.* Seattle: Bay Press, 1992, 285–291.

Dike, Virginia. "Developing Fiction for Today's Nigerian Youth." *Sankofa: Journal of African Children and Young Adult Literature* 6 (2005): 6–17.

Dixon, Melvin. "The Black Writer's use of Memory." In Genevieve Fabre and Robert O'Meally (eds.), *History and Memory in African-American Culture.* New York: Oxford University Press, 1994, 18–27.

Du Bois, W. E. B. *The World and Africa: An Inquiry into the Part which Africa has Played in World History.* New York: International Publishers, 1992.

During, Simon. "Postmodern or Postcolonialism Today." In B. Ashcroft, G. Griffith, & H. Tiffin (eds.), *The Postcolonial Studies Reader.* London: Routledge, 1992, 125–129.

Ethnic Notions: Black People in White Minds. Producer/Director: Marlon Riggs. San Francisco: California Newsreel, 1987.

Fee, M. "*Who* can write as other?" In B. Ashcroft, G. Griffiths, & H. Tiffin (eds.), *The Post-colonial Studies Reader*. London: Routledge, 1995, 242–245.

Feierman, Steven. "Africa in History: The End of Universal Narrative." In Gyan Prakash (ed.), *After Colonialism: Imperial Histories and Postcolonial Displacements*. Princeton, NJ: Princeton University Press, 1995, 40–65.

Freeman, E. & Lehman, Barbara. *Global Perspectives in Children's Literature*. Boston, MA: Allyn and Bacon, 2001.

Giroux, H. A. "Paulo Freire and the Politics of Postcolonialism." *Journal of Advanced Composition* 12(1) (1992): 15–25.

The Gods Must Be Crazy. Twentieth Century-Fox. A C.A.T. Films Production. 1986.

Goldberg, D. *Racist Culture: Philosophy and the Politics of Meaning*. Oxford: Blackwell, 1993.

Granqvist, Raoul. "Who Is Building the House?: Myth, Nation and Culture in African and Caribbean Children's Literatures." In Raoul Granqvist and Jurgen Martini (eds.), *Preserving the Landscape of Imagination: Children's Literature in Africa*. Atlanta, GA: Rodopi, 1997. 22–41.

Granqvist, R. & Martini, J. *Preserving the Landscape of Imagination: Children's Literature in Africa*. Atlanta, GA: Rodopi, 1997.

Gray, S. "Nigeria On-screen: 'Nollywood Films' Popularity Rising Among Emigres." Washingtonpost.com. 2003. Accessed April 28, 2004.

Grifalconi, Ann. *The Village That Vanished*. Illus. Kadir Nelson. New York: Dial, 2002. H-Afrteach web site: http://www.h-net.msu.edu/~afrteach/.

Guru, Wangui Wa. "Publishing, Teaching, Evaluation and Review in Translation Theory and Practices: Perspectives on an Emerging Canon." Madison, WI: African Literature Association, 2004.

Hogan, Patrick C. *Colonialism and Cultural Identity*. New York: State University of New York Press, 2000.

Hollindale, Peter. "Ideology and the Children's Book." *Literature for Children: Contemporary Criticism*. London, New York: Routledge, 1992, 18–34.

Holtorf, Cornelius. "Cultural Memory." At http://tspace.library.utoronto.ca/citd/holtorf/2.0.html. 2002. Accessed June 28, 2005.

hooks, b. *Black Looks: Race and Representation*. Boston, MA: South End Press, 1992.

———. *Killing Rage: Ending Racism*. New York: Owl Books, 1995.

———. *Outlaw Culture: Resisting Representations*. New York: Routledge, 1994.

———. *Sisters of the Yam*. Boston: South End Press, 2005.

———. *Teaching To Transgress: Education as the Practice of Freedom*. New York: Routledge, 1994.

The Horn Book Guide Online. At http://gw2.scbbs.com/Hbook/hornbook.jsp?. Accessed July 13, 2004.

Hunt, P. *Literature for Children: Contemporary Criticism*. London: Routledge, 1993.

I Dreamed of Africa. Directed by Hugh Hudson. Produced by Stanley R. Jaffe. 2000.

Irele, A. " Dimensions of African Discourse." In K. Mysiades and J. Mcguire (eds.), *Order and Partialities*. Albany, NY: SUNY Press, 1995, 15–34.

Jacobs, James & Tunnell, Michael. *Children's Literature, Briefly*. Columbus, OH: Merrill Prentice Hall, 2004.

Jones, H. *Mutiny on the Amistad*. Oxford: Oxford University Press, 1987.

Kauffman, J. "T. Obinkaram Echewa: Telling Stories in Three Dimensions." An interview at http://www.rambles.net/echewa_stories.html. 1995. Accessed March 2, 2005.

Khorana, M. *Africa in Literature for Children and Young Adults: An Annotated Bibliography of English-language Books*. Westport, CT: Greenwood Press, 1994.

———. "Children's Publishing in Africa: Can the Colonial Past Be Forgotten?" In Meena Khorana (ed.), *Critical Perspectives on Postcolonial African Children's and Young Adult Literature*. Westport, CT: Greenwood Press, 1998, 1–13.

———. *Critical Perspectives on Postcolonial African Children's and Young Adult Literature*. Westport, CT: Greenwood Press, 1998.

Kimble-Ellis, S. "Sosu's Call." *Black Issues Book Review*. 2002. At http://www.findarticles.com. Accessed April 12, 2004.

King Solomon's Mines. Voyager, 1937.

Kirkpatrick, Mary Alice. "Documenting the American South: Charles Waddell Chestnutt, 1858–1932. The Conjure Woman. Boston and New York: Houghton, Mifflin and Company, 1899." 2004. At http://docsouth.unc.edu/chestnuttconjure/summary.html. Accessed May 16, 2005.

Kirkus Review. 1999. Amazon.com. Accessed April 13, 2004.

Klein, H. *The Atlantic Slave Trade*. New York: Cambridge University Press, 1999.

Kolawole, M. *Womanism and African Consciousness.* Trenton: Africa World Press, 1997.

Kotei, S. "The Book Today in Africa." In B. Ashcroft, G. Griffiths, & H. Tiffin (eds.), *The Post-colonial Studies Reader.* London: Routledge, 1995, 480–484.

Larson, C. "Cyprian Ekwensi." *Bellagio Publishing Network Newsletter.* Issue No. 29. At bellagio publishingnetwork.org/newsletter29/larsonhtml. 2001. Accessed April 10, 2004.

———. *The Ordeal of the African Writer.* London: Zed Books, 2001.

"Leo and Diane Dillon." CBC Book Council. 2004. At http://cbcbooks.org/html/leo_and_diane_dillon.html. Accessed March 5, 2004. "Leo Dillon's Interview + Transcript." At www2.scholastic.com/teachers/authorsandbooks/authorstudies/authorhome.jhtml?authorID=111 17&displayname=interview%2Btranscript. Accessed March 5, 2004.

Lindfors, B. *Africa Talks Back: Interviews with Anglophone African Authors.* Trenton, NJ: Africa World Press, 2002.

MacCann, D. *Apartheid and Racism in South African Children's Literature, 1985–1995.* London: Routledge, 2001.

———. "Review of Pierre Yves Njeng, *Vacation in the Village.*" H-AfrTeach, H-Net Reviews, March 2000.

MacCann, D. & Maddy, A. Y. *African Images in Juvenile Literature: Commentaries on Neocolonialist Fiction.* Jefferson, NC: McFarland and Company, 1996.

MacCann, D. & Richard, O. "Through African Eyes: An Interview about Recent Picture Books with Yulisa Amadu Maddy." *Wilson Library Bulletin* 69.10 (June 1995): 41–45, 141.

Maddy, Yulisa Amadu & MacCann, Donnarae. "Anti-African Themes in 'Liberal' Young Adult Novels." *Children's Literature Association Quarterly* 27.2 (2002): 92–99.

Marable, M. (1992). "Race, Identity, and Political Culture." In G. Dent (ed.), *Black Popular Culture.* Seattle: Bay Press, 285–291.

Martin, M. *Brown Gold: Milestones of African-American Children's Picture Books, 1845–2002.* New York: Routledge, 2004.

Martin, Michele H. "Postmodern Periods: Menstruation Media in the 1990s." *The Lion and the Unicorn* 23.3 (1999): 395–414. At http://muse.jhu.edu/journals/lion_and_the_unicorn/v023/23.3/martin.html. Accessed January 4, 2006.

Marton, D. "Review of *Madoulina: A Girl Who Wanted to Go to School.*" *The School Library.* 1999. Amazon.com. Accessed April 13, 2004.

Mbiti, J. S. *African Religions and Philosophy.* Second Edition. London: Heinemann, 1989.

McElmeel, Sharron L. *100 Most Popular Picture Book Authors and Illustrators: Biographical Sketches and Bibliographies.* Englewood, CO: Libraries Unlimited, 2000.

Mhlophe, Gcina. "The 'Story' the Mother of Creativity." *Sankofa: A Journal of African Children's and Young Adult Literature* 2 (2003): 6–12.

Trinh Minh-ha. "Not You/Like You." 1997. At http://www.colorado.edu/English/ENGL2012Klages/trinh.html. Accessed October 4, 2005.

———. "Not You/Like You: Post-colonial Women and the Interlocking Questions of Identity and Difference." 1998. At http://humwww.ucsc.edu/CultStudies/PUBS/Inscriptions/vol_3-4/minh-ha.html. Accessed October 4, 2005.

———. *Woman, Native, Other: Writing Postcoloniality and Feminism.* Indianapolis, IN: Indiana University Press, 1989.

———. "Writing Postcoloniality and Feminism." In B. Ashcroft, G. Griffiths, & H. Tiffin (eds.), *The Post-colonial Studies Reader.* London: Routledge, 1995, 264–268.

Moore, Leslie. "Sense Pass King." 2003. H-Afrteach web site: http://www.h-net.org/reviews/showrev.cgi?path=218561054017156.

Motherland: A Genetic Journey. Director: T. Jackson & A. Brown. Takeaway Media. Sundance Television Channel. 2003. Viewed November 22, 2004.

Multi Murders: The Dark Side of Occult Belief Systems in Africa. Director: Olivier Becker. Producer: Helmut Fischer. A Production of Occasions. Sundance Channel. 2004.

"Mutiny (Slave Rebellion)." *The Great Blacks in Wax Museum.* Baltimore, MD. September 2005.

Myers, J. "The Value-Laden Assumptions of our Interpretive Practices." *Reading Research Quarterly* 30.3 (1995): 582–587.

Ngugi wa Thiong'o. *The River Between.* Portsmouth, NH: Heinemann, 1972.

———. *Writers in Politics.* Portsmouth, NH: Heinemann, 1997.

Norton, D. *Multicultural Children's Literature.* Second Edition. Columbus, OH: Pearson, 2005.

Nwapa, Flora. "Writing and Publishing for Children in Africa—A Personal Account." In Raoul Granqvist and Jurgen Martini (eds.), *Preserving the Landscape of Imagination: Children's Literature in Africa.* Atlanta, GA: Rodopi, 1997, 265–275.

Nyamnjoh, F. "From Publish or Perish to Publish and Perish: What Africa's 100 Best Books Tell Us About Publishing Africa." 2004. At http://www.sabdet.com/Nyamnjoh%20ASAUK%20% 20doc. pdf. Accessed June 23, 2005.

Obiechina, E. *Culture, Tradition and Society in the West African Novel.* Cambridge: Cambridge University Press, 1975.

Ogot, G. "The Rain Came." In Charlotte H. Bruner (ed.), *Unwinding Threads.* Nigeria: Heinemann Educational Books, 1983, 91–99.

O'Reilly, Andrea & Abbey, Sharon. "Introduction." *Mothers and Daughters.* New York: Rowman and Littlefield, 2000, 1–18.

Osa, O. *African Children's and Youth Literature.* New York: Twayne Publishers, 1995.

——. "Preserving the Landscape of the Imagination: Children's Literature in Africa, ed. Raoul Granqvist and Jurgen Martini. Amsterdam: Rodopi, 1997." In *Research in African Literatures* (1998): 166–171. Passport.imaginarylands.org/continents/Africa.html. Accessed November 2005.

Out of Africa. Universal Pictures. New York: Mirage Enterprise Production, 1986.

Oyebade, Bayo. "African Studies and the Afrocentric Paradigm—A Critique." *Journal of Black Studies* 21(2): 233–238. At http://www.jstor.org. Accessed November 3, 2003.

Parker, Farris. "Establishing Roots: African-American Images, Past and Present." 1996. At http://www.scils.rutgers.edu/~kvander/books/PARKER.pdf. Accessed May 14, 2004.

Paul, Lissa. "Sex and the Children's Book." *The Lion and the Unicorn* 29.2 (2005): 222–235.

Paye-Layleh, J. "Liberian 'Ritual Killings' Alert." BBC News. 2005. At http://news.bbc.co.uk/go/ pr/fr/-/2/hi/africa/4205301.stm. Accessed June 20, 2005.

Peirce, B. N. "Toward a pedagogy of possibility in the teaching of English internationally: People's English in South Africa." In P. Shannon (ed.), *Becoming Political: Readings and Writings in the Politics of Literacy Education.* Portsmouth, NH: Heinemann, 1992, 155–170.

Philips, J. "The African Heritage of White America." In J. Holloway (ed.), *Africanisms in American Culture.* Bloomington, IN.: Indiana University Press, 1990, 225–230.

Prakash, Gyan. "Introduction." In *After Colonialism: Imperial Histories and Postcolonial Displacements.* Princeton, NJ: Princeton University Press, 1995, 3–17.

Punter, D. *Postcolonial Imaginings: Fictions of a New World Order.* London: Rowman and Littlefield, 2000.

Randolph, Brenda. "Children's Africana Book Awards 2003: The Publishing Year 2002." *Sankofa: A Journal of African Children's and Young Adult Literature* 2 (2003): 62–70.

Reyes, Angelita. *Mothering Across Cultures.* Minneapolis: University of Minnesota Press, 2002.

Schmidt, N. *Children's Books on Africa and their Authors: An Annotated Bibliography.* New York: Africana Publishing Company, 1975.

——. "Resources on African Literature: Children's Literature." In T. Hale and R. Priebe (eds.), Washington, DC: Three Continent Press, 1989, 125–147.

Scott, G. *Come With Me to Africa: A Photographic Journey.* New York: Kreikmeier, Golden Books, 1993.

Segun, Mabel. "Illustrating for Children." In Raoul Granqvist and Jurgen Martini (eds.), *Preserving the Landscape of Imagination: Children's Literature in Africa.* Atlanta, GA: Rodopi, 1997, 76–89.

Shannon, P. *Text, Lies, and Videotape: Stories about Life, Literacy, and Learning.* Portsmouth, NH: Heinemann, 1995.

Sheffer, Susannah. "Adolescent Girls and Sexual Desire." 1997. At http://www.findarticles.com. Accessed January 31, 2005.

Simon, R. "Empowerment as a Pedagogy of Possibility." In P. Shannon (ed.), *Becoming Political: Readings and Writings in the Politics of Literacy Education.* Portsmouth, NH: Heinemann, 1992, 139–151.

Sims, R. *Shadow and Substance: Afro-American Experience In Contemporary Children's Fiction.* Urbana, IL: NCTE, 1982.

——. "What Has Happened to the 'All-White' World of Children's Books?" *Phi Delta Kappan* 64.9 (May 1983): 650–653.

Sindima, Harvey. "Liberalism and African Culture." *Journal of Black Studies* 21.2 (1990): 190–209. At http://www.jstor.org. Accessed November 13, 2003.

Slapin, B. & Seale, D. *Through Indian Eyes: The Native Experience in Books for Children.* Philadelphia: New Society Publishers, 1992.

Smith, Valerie. "Black Feminist Theory and the Representation of the Other." In Robyn R. Warhol and Diane Price Hemdll (eds.), *Feminisms: An Anthology of Literary Theory and Criticism.* New Brunswick: Rutgers University Press, 1997, 311–325.

Soffield, H. "Postcolonial Identity, Postcolonial Literature." At http://postcolonialweb.org/zimbabwe/sofiel/6.html. 1999. Accessed July 2, 2004.

Spitz, Ellen Handler. *Inside Picture Books*. New Haven, CT: Yale University Press, 1999.

Spivak, G. *The Post-colonial Critic: Interviews, Strategies, Dialogues*. New York: Routledge, 1990.

Stoehr, Shelley. "Controversial Issues in the Lives of Contemporary Young Adults." *The ALAN Review* 24(2, Winter 1997). At http://Scholar.lib.vt.edu/ejournals/ALAN/winter97/w97-02-stoehr.html. Accessed December 20, 2004.

Strom, S. "How a Goat Led a Girl Up the Path to an Education." *New York Times*, January 25, 2004: 11.

60 Minutes. "Beatrice's Goat." Produced by Reneé Kaplan and Joel Bernstein. WYOU Local Channel 22. June 12, 2005.

Tadjo, Veronique. "The Challenges of Publishing for Children in French-speaking Africa: The Cote d'Ivoire Example." *Sankofa: Journal of African Children's and Young Adult Literature* 4 (2005): 18–22.

Tarbinlam Nguni. " 'African Village' Exhibit in Zoo, Augsburg: July 9th–12th 2005." E-mail correspondence to Yahoo group BFU-USA (Bui Family Union). June 2, 2005.

Tate, Claudia. "A Usable Future for Literary Studies." Presented at the English Association of the Pennsylvania State Universities, Millersville University, October 16, 1999.

——. *Domestic Allegories of Political Desire*. New York: Oxford University Press, 1992.

Thomas, H. *The Slave Trade: The Story of the Atlantic Slave Trade: 1440–1870*. New York: Simon and Schuster, 1997.

Thompson, R. "Kongo Influences on African-American Artistic Culture." In J. Holloway (ed.), *Africanisms in American Culture*. Bloomington, IN: Indiana University Press, 1990, 148–184.

Thornton, J. *Africa and Africans in the Making of the Atlantic World, 1400–1800*. Second Edition. Cambridge: Cambridge University Press, 1998.

Treiber, Jeanette. "Feminism and Identity Politics: Mariama Ba's *Un Chant Ecarlate*." *Research in African Literature* 27.4 (1996): 109–123.

Tugend, A. "A Scholar Examines Colonial Images in British Children's Literature." *The Chronicle of Higher Education* 43.20 (1997): Al2, A14.

Turner, J. "The Continuing Legacy of Excellence in Scholarship." Africana Research Workshop, Bloomsburg University, 2005.

Ungar, S. J. *Africa: The People and Politics of an Emerging Continent*. New York: Simon & Schuster, 1986.

Vawter, N. "Author Explores Faith and Country in Acclaimed New Novel" (Interview). October 13, 2004. At http://allafrica.com/stories/200410130920html. Accessed April 18, 2005.

Walker, Alice. *In Search of Our Mother's Gardens*. New York: Harcourt, 1983.

Ward, Cynthia. "Reading African Women Readers." *Research in African Literature* 27.3 (1996): 78–86.

Winkler, K. "An African Writer at a Crossroads." *Chronicle of Higher Education* 40.19 (January 12, 1994): A9, A12.

Wisker, Gina. *Post-colonial and African Women's Writing*. New York: St. Martin's Press, 2000.

Wonham, H. *Playing the Races: Ethnic Caricature and American Literary Realism*. New York: Oxford University Press, 2004.

Woodson, Jacqueline. "Who Can Tell My Story?" *Horn Book Magazine* 74.1 (1998): 34–38.

Zipes, Jack. *The Trials and Tribulations of Little Red Riding Hood*. London: Routledge, 1993.

Children's Books Cited

Aardema, V. *Anansi Finds a Fool*. Illustrated by Bryna Waldman. New York: Dial Press, 1992.

——. *Tales for the Third Ear*. Drawings by Ib Ohlsson. New York: Dutton, 1969.

——. *The Na of Wa*. Illustrated by Elton Fax. New York: Coward-McCann, 1960.

——. *Why Mosquitoes Buzz in People's Ears*. Illustrated by Leo and Diane Dillon. New York: Dial Press, 1975.

Achebe, C. & Iroaganachi, J. *How Leopard Got Its Claws*. Enugu, Nigeria: Nwanife Publishers, 1972.

Alexander, Lloyd. *The Fortune-Tellers*. Illustrated by Trina Schart Hyman. New York: Dutton, 1992.

Anderson, D. *The Origin of Life on Earth: An African Creation Myth*. Illustrated by Kathleen Atkins Wilson. Mt. Airy, MD: Sights Press, 1991.

Appiah, P. *Gift of the Mmoatia*. Ghana: Tema, 1972.

Arkhurst, J. *The Adventures of Spider: West African Folktales*. Boston, MA: Little, Brown & Co., 1964.

Asare, M. *Meliga's Day*. Ghana: Sub-Saharan Publishers. 2000.

——. *Sosu's Call.* California: Kane/Miller, 2002.

Atta, Sefi. *Everything Good will Come.* Massachusetts: Interlink, 2005.

Bedford, R. *Yoruba Girl Dancing.* London: Longman, 1992.

Belton, Sandra. *Beauty, Her Basket.* Illustrated by A. Cabera Cozbi. New York: HarperCollins, 2004.

Blume, Judy. *Forever.* New York: Pocket Books, 1975.

Bognomo, E. *Madoulina: A Girl Who Wanted to Go to School.* Honesdale, PA: Boyds Mill Press, 1999.

Bryan, A. *Beat the Story Drum, Pum-Pum.* New York: Atheneum, 1987.

Burnett, F. *The Secret Garden.* New York: Dell-Yearling Books, 1987.

Burns, Khephra. *Mansa Musa: A Lion in Mali.* Illustrated by Leo Dillon and Diane Dillon. San Diego: Gulliver Books, 2001.

Burton, W. *The Magic Drum.* New York: Criterion Books, 1961.

Bynum, E. *Jamari's Drum.* Illustrated by Baba Wagué Diakité. Toronto: A Groundwood Book, 2004.

Chambers, Aidan. *Postcards from No Man's Land.* London: Red Fox, 2001.

Clifford, M. L. *Salah of Sierra Leone.* New York: Crowell, 1975.

Clifton, L. (1973). *All Us Come Cross the Water.* Illustrated by John Steptoe. New York: Holt, Reinhart, & Winston, 1973.

Courlander, H. & Herzog, G. *The Cow-Tail Switch and Other West African Stories.* Illustrated by Madye Lee Chastian. New York: Henry Holt, 1947.

Cowen-Fletcher, J. *It Takes a Village.* New York: Scholastic, 1994.

Crutcher, Chris. *Chinese Handcuffs.* New York: Laurel-Leaf, 1989.

Dangaremgba, Tsitsi. *Nervous Conditions.* Seattle: Seal, 1992.

Dawes, K. *I Saw Your Face.* Illustrated by Tom Feelings. New York: Dial Books, 2005.

Dayrell, E. *Why the Sun and Moon Live in the Sky.* Boston, MA: Houghton Mifflin, 1968.

Dee, R. *Two Ways to Count to Ten.* Illustrated by Susan Meddaugh. New York: Henry Holt, 1988.

Diakité, B. *The Hatseller and the Monkeys.* New York: Scholastic, 1999.

——. *The Magic Gourd.* New York: 2003.

Easmon, C. *Bisi and the Golden Disc.* New York: Crocodile, 1990.

Echewa, T. Obinkaram. *The Ancestor Tree.* Illustrated by Christy Hale. New York: Lodestar Books, 1994.

Ekeh, E. *How Tables Came to Umu Madu: The Fabulous History of an Unknown Continent.* Trenton, NJ: Africa World Press, 1989.

Ekwensi, Cyprian. *Juju rock.* Lagos, Nigeria: African University Press, 1966.

——. *Motherless Baby.* Nigeria: Heinemann Educational Books, 2001.

——. *The Drummer Boy.* Ibadan, Nigeria: Heinemann, 1967/1988.

Ellis, Deborah. *The Heaven Shop.* Massachusetts: Fitzhenry & Whitehead, 2004.

Emecheta, Buchi. *The Bride Price.* New York: George Braziller, 1976.

——. *The Rape of Shavi.* New York: George Brazillier, 1985.

Feelings, Tom. *The Middle Passage: White Ships/Black Cargo.* New York: Dial Books, 1995.

——. *Soul Looks Back in Wonder.* New York: Dial Books, 1993.

Franklin, K. L. *The Old, Old Man and the Very Little Boy.* Illustrated by T. D. Shaffer. New York: Atheneum, 1992.

Gerson, M. *Why the Sky is Far Away: A Nigerian Folktale.* Pictures by Carla Golembe 1992.

Giovanni, Nikki. *Ego-tripping and Other Poems for Young People.* Illustrated by George Ford. New York: Lawrence Hills Books, 1993.

Gray, N. *A Country Far Away.* Illustrated by P. Dupasquier. New York: Orchard, 1989.

Greenfield, Eloise. *Africa Dream.* Illustrated by Carole Byard. New York: HarperCollins, 1977.

Green, L. *Folktales and Fairy Tales of Africa.* Illustrated by J. P. Silver. 1967.

Grifalconi, A. *Darkness and the Butterfly.* Boston: Little Brown & Co., 1987.

——. *Flyaway Girl.* Boston: Little, Brown & Co., 1992.

——. *Osa's Pride.* Boston: Little, Brown & Co., 1990.

——. *The Village of Round and Square Houses.* Boston: Little Brown & Co., 1986.

Haley, G. E. *A Story, A Story: An African Tale.* New York: Aladdin Books, 1970.

Hamilton, Virginia. *The People Could Fly.* Illustrated by Leo and Diane Dillon. New York: Alfred Knopf, 2004.

——. *Zeely.* Illustrated by Symeon Shimin. New York: Macmillan, 1967.

Hartmann, W. *One Sun Rises: An African Wildlife Counting Book.* Illustrated by Nicolaas Maritz. New York: Dutton Children's Books, 1994.

Haskett, E. (ed.). *Some Gold, A Little Ivory.* New York: John Day, 1971.

Hoffman, M. *Boundless Grace.* Illustrated by C. Binch. New York: Dial Books, 1995.

Joose, B. *Papa, Do You Love Me?* Illustrated by Barbara Lavallee. San Francisco: Chronicle Books, 2005.

Keita, F. *The Smile Stealer.* Illustrated by Claire Mobio. Translated by Adrian Murphy. Abidjan: Nouvelles Editions Ivoiriennes, 1996.

Kessler, Cristina. *No Condition is Permanent.* New York: Philomel, 2000.

——. *Our Secret, Siri Aang.* New York: Philomel, 2004.

Kimmel, E. *Anansi and the Moss-covered Rock.* Illustrated by Janet Stevens. New York: Holiday House, 1988.

——. *Anansi Goes Fishing.* New York: Holiday House, 1992.

Knight, M. B. & Melniove, Mark. *Africa is Not a Country.* Illustrated by Anne Sibley O'Brien. Connecticut: Millbrook Press, 2000

Kroll, V. *Africa: Brothers and Sisters.* Illustrated by Vanessa French. New York: Aladdin Books, 1993.

——. *An African Mother Goose.* Illustrated by Katherine Roundtree. Massachusetts: Charlesbridge, 1995.

——. *Jaha and Jamil Went Down the Hill.* Illustrated by Katherine Roundtree. MA: Charlesbridge, 1995.

LaTeef, Nelda. *The Hunter and the Ebony Tree.* North Kingstown, RI: Moon Mountain, 2002.

Lester, J. *How Many Spots Does a Leopard Have and Other Tales.* Illustrated by David Shannon. New York: Scholastic, 1989.

Mandela, N. *Favorite African Folktales.* New York: W. W. Norton & Company, 2002.

McBrier, P. *Beatrice's Goat.* Illustrated by Lori Lohstoeter. New York: Aladdin Paperbacks, 2001.

McDermott, G. *Anansi the Spider: A Tale from the Ashanti.* 1972.

Medearis, A. *Too Much Talk.* Illustrated by Stefano Vitale. New York: Candlewick Press, 1995.

Mendez, P. *The Black Snowman.* Illustrated by C. M. Byard. New York: Scholastic, 1989.

Musgrove, Margaret. *Ashanti to Zulu: African Traditions.* Illustrated by Leo Dillon and Diane Dillon. New York: Dial, 1976.

Mwangi, M. *Kill Me Quick.* London: Heinemann, 1973.

Njeng, P. *Vacation in the Village.* Honesdale, PA: Boyds Mill Press, 1999.

Olaleye, I. *Bitter Bananas.* Illustrated by E. Young. Honesdale, PA: Boyds Mills Press, 1994.

—— *The Distant Talking Drum.* Paintings by Frane Lessac. Honesdale, PA: Wordsong/Boyds Mills Press, 1995.

Onyefulu, I. *A is for Africa.* New York: Cobblehill Books/Dutton, 1993.

——. *Emeka's Gift: An African Counting Story.* New York: Cobblehill Books, 1995.

Owoo, I. *A is for Africa.* Lawrencevill, NJ: Africa World Press, 1992.

Oyono, E. *Gollo and the Lion.* Illustrated by Laurent Corvaissier. New York: Hyperion, 1995.

Pryce, Leontyne. *Aida.* Illustrated by Leo Dillon and Diane Dillon. New York: Voyager Books, 1990.

Raven, Margot Theis. *Circle Unbroken: The Story of a Basket and Its People.* Illustrated by E. B Lewis. New York: Melanie Kroupa Books, 2004.

Saphire. *Push.* New York: Vintage, 1997.

Scoppettone, Sandra. *Happy Endings are All Alike.* Boston: Alyson Publications, 1978.

Siegelson, K. *In the Time of the Drums.* Illustrated by Brian Pinkney. New York: Hyperion Books, 1999.

Smalls, Irene. *Ebony Sea.* Illustrated by Jon Lockard. Stanford, CT: Longmeadow Press, 1995.

Steig, W. *Doctor De Soto goes to Africa.* New York: HarperCollins, 1992.

Steptoe, John. *Birthday.* New York: Henry Holt, 1972.

Stratton, Allan. *Chanda's Secret.* Toronto: Annick Press, 2004.

Tadjo, V. *Mamy Wata and the Monster.* Abidjan: Nouvelles Editions Ivoiriennes, 1997.

Tchana, Katrin Hyman. *Sense Pass King.* Illustrated by Trina Schart Hyman. New York: Holiday House, 2002.

Tchana, K. & L. Pami. *Oh, No, Toto!* Illustrated by Colin Bootman. New York: Scholastic, 1997.

Tutuola, A. *Ajaiyi and His Inherited Poverty.* London: Faber, 1967.

Unobagha, U. *Off to the Sweet Shores of Africa: And Other Talking Drum Rhymes.* Illustrated by Julia Cairns. San Francisco: Chronicle Books, 2000.

Walker, B. *The Dancing Palm Tree and Other Nigerian Folktales.* Woodcuts by Helen Seigle. Texas: Texas Tech University Press, 1990.

Watson, P. *The Heart of the Lion.* Illustrated by M. Watson. New Jersey: Shenanigan Books, 2005.

—— *The Market Lady and the Mango Tree.* Illustrated by M. Watson. New York: Tambourine Books, 1994.

Williams-Garcia, Rita. *No Laughter Here*. New York: HarperCollins, 2004.
Williams, K. L. *When Africa was Home*. Illustrated by F. Cooper. New York: Orchard, 1991.
Wilson, B. *The Great Minu*. Illustrated by Jerry Pinkney. Chicago: Follet Publishing, 1974.
Zimelman, N. *Treed by a Pride of Irate Lions*. Boston: Little, Brown & Co., 1990.

Index

Date Due

FEB 0 4 2008			

PRINTED IN U.S.A.   CAT. NO. 24-161   BRO DART